Appraisal and Evaluation
IT Infrastructure Library

IT Service Delivery Tools

LONDON: HMSO

Acknowledgements CCTA is grateful for the assistance of David Wheeldon of Ultracomp Ltd in the preparation of this volume.

During research and writing of the volume, valuable contributions were made by David Bell of Ultracomp Ltd, Chris Edmonds of IT Southern, Adam Grummitt of Metron Technology Ltd, Alex McDonald of Legent Plc and Tim Robinson of Computer Associates.

© Crown copyright 1996

Applications for reproduction should be made to HMSO's Copyright Unit

ISBN 0 11 330633 4

For further information regarding CCTA products please contact:

CCTA Library
Rosebery Court
St Andrews Business Park
Norwich
NR7 0HS
01603 704930

Contents

Chapter		Page
1	**General**	7
	1.1 Background	
	1.2 The importance of service delivery tools	
	1.3 Readership	
	1.4 Expected uses	
	1.5 Structure of this volume	
	1.6 Outline of the procedure	
2	**Scope**	13
	2.1 Service delivery definition	
	2.2 Service delivery tools	
	2.3 Terminology	
3	**Criteria**	17
	3.1 Notation	
	3.2 Summary of the criteria	
	3.3 Questions	
4	**Conformity with the IT Infrastructure Library**	21
	4.1 Service level management	
	4.2 Cost management for IT services	
	4.3 Contingency planning	
	4.4 Capacity management	
	4.5 Availability management	
5	**Monitoring**	41
	5.1 Monitoring details	
	5.2 Monitoring of customer service	
6	**Data structure and handling**	47
	6.1 Data definition and data flow	
	6.2 Data definition modification	
	6.3 Data manipulation	
	6.4 Standards	
7	**Integration with other products**	59
	7.1 Service level management	
	7.2 Cost management	
	7.3 Contingency planning	
	7.4 Capacity management	
	7.5 Availability management	
Annex A	**Criteria hierarchy**	73
Annex B	**Evaluation checklist**	77
Annex C	**Glossary**	85

Part 1
Introduction

1 General

1.1 Background

This volume is concerned with IT infrastructure service delivery tools appraisal and evaluation. Service delivery, as defined in the CCTA IT Infrastructure Library (ITIL) consists of the following functions which are covered in separate books in the *Service Delivery Set* of the Library:

- *Service Level Management*
- *Cost Management for IT Services*
- *Contingency Planning*
- *Capacity Management*
- *Availability Management.*

For an overview of the contents and aims of the IT Infrastructure Library there is a free booklet called *The IT Infrastructure Library – An Introduction*. The IT Infrastructure Library is managed (on behalf of CCTA) by EXIN. For more information on ITIL contact EXIN at:

> Room 6S11
> Sovereign House
> Botolph Street
> Norwich
> NR3 1DN
>
> Telephone: (01603) 695172
> Fax: (01603) 695174
> Email address: itil@exin.nl

The objective of the Appraisal and Evaluation Library is to define a framework for

> **...impartial and effective evaluation to find the product, or products, which best meet the needs and constraints of the organisation.**

Continually adapting to changes in software and technology, the Appraisal and Evaluation Library has been added to over time. In 1992 the first volume produced for IT Infrastructure Management called *IT Infrastructure Support Tools* was added to the Library. This is the second volume covering IT Infrastructure Management and is a sister volume to *IT Infrastructure Support Tools*. We welcome feedback on the ease of use of this volume and on the desirability of further volumes to underpin the IT Infrastructure Library.

1.2 The importance of service delivery tools

Among the trends facing IT services management are:

- more sophisticated end user demands
- IT skill shortages and budget constraints
- increasing business reliance on IT systems and hence focus on IT service quality
- an increasing tendency to contract out IT service provision to an external provider (possibly as a result of market testing exercises)
- integration of multi-vendor environments
- IT infrastructures that are becoming more complex to manage
- emergence of international standards
- increasing range and frequency of change to hardware, software and telecommunications.

To help IT service managers cope with these trends, CCTA has produced written guidance based on the best IT practices within the private and public sectors – the IT Infrastructure Library. The Library is divided into nine sets of books:

- *The Manager's Set*
- *Service Delivery Set*
- *Service Support Set*
- *Computer Operations Set*
- *Software Support Set*
- *Networks Set*
- *Environmental Strategy Set*
- *Office Environment Set*
- *Environmental Management Set.*

This volume underpins the *Service Delivery Set*. The set consists of the five books referred to in section 1.1. Additionally, a number of other books, covering complimentary topics have been written; these include *A Guide to Business Continuity Management* and *ITIL in*

Chapter 1
General

Small IT Units. For further information, please contact EXIN at the address given in section 1.1.

The use of automated tools in IT services management has become critical as the requirements for managing current and future processing architectures have increased in complexity. Service delivery tools can provide improved efficiency and effectiveness in the areas of service level, cost, capacity, availability management and contingency planning.

These tools can centralise or automate routine operations and improve the quality and availability of information used to manage the IT infrastructure (ie the hardware, software and communications upon which the application systems and IT services are built and run). Without automated support tools the tasks associated with IT service delivery are very time consuming, expensive, difficult or in some cases impossible, to achieve.

Automated tools for service delivery will be of even greater benefit if they are closely coupled to, or better still are fully integrated with, support tools for service support and other service management disciplines.

Despite the pressures on the IT infrastructure management function it is possible to continue to meet end user expectations of functionality and reliability and still maintain cost-effectiveness. In order to do this the IT service provider will have to implement best practices in all areas. The automation of core functions will be a major objective but this must be accompanied by adequate organisational procedures, management commitment and clear infrastructure planning that is coherent with the organisation's overall policy of system architecture.

1.3 Readership

The main readership for this volume is IT staff wishing to carry out appraisals or evaluations for the soundly based procurement of support tools for service delivery. The developers of such tools will also find the volume useful as a guide to the type of features that potential customers will be seeking.

It is assumed that the reader has at least a basic understanding of information processing and of hardware and software architecture. Some knowledge of service delivery requirements will be essential and the reader should consult the *Service Delivery Set* of the IT Infrastructure Library to become familiar with the core support functions.

Because of these assumptions, experienced infrastructure management practitioners may find the volume descriptive in parts, but technically simplified in others. It should be remembered, however, that it can be used as a primer for those unfamiliar with the topic, while also serving as a useful reference document for those who are more experienced.

1.4 Expected uses

It is expected that volumes in the Appraisal and Evaluation Library will be used in several ways. Uses identified in the *Overview and Procedures* volume are:

- strategic, business-based, evaluation of products to select a product for subsequent organisation-wide use
- less detailed evaluation of products as an element of a feasibility study
- full evaluation of products during procurement for a project
- independent appraisal of a product.

Readers of the IT Infrastructure Library can use this volume to evaluate the tools required to support the functions described in the *Service Delivery Set* of the Library. In addition, the volume can be used by software suppliers as a guide to the type of features that potential customers will be looking for in automated service delivery tools.

1.5 Structure of this volume

This volume comprises three parts: Part 1 – *Introduction*, Part 2 – *The Evaluation Criteria*, and Part 3 – *Annexes*.

This section introduces the volume as a whole. Chapter 2 describes the scope of the subject area and explains the terminology. Chapter 3 describes the notation used for the criteria and summarises the main headings.

The bulk of the volume contains the high-level criteria and the checklist of detailed technical and functional questions used within the evaluation model to assess and rank service delivery tools. The questions can be used as an *aide-mémoire* when gathering information about products or in establishing a detailed Operational Requirement.

Annex A contains a hierarchy chart of the subject matter in this volume. This chart may be used as a default or as the basis of a hierarchy chart which best meets the needs of the organisation. Annex B provides a checklist of selection criteria taken from the main body of the text.

1.6 Outline of the procedure

The evaluation process comprises seven stages which are described in the *Overview and Procedures* volume.

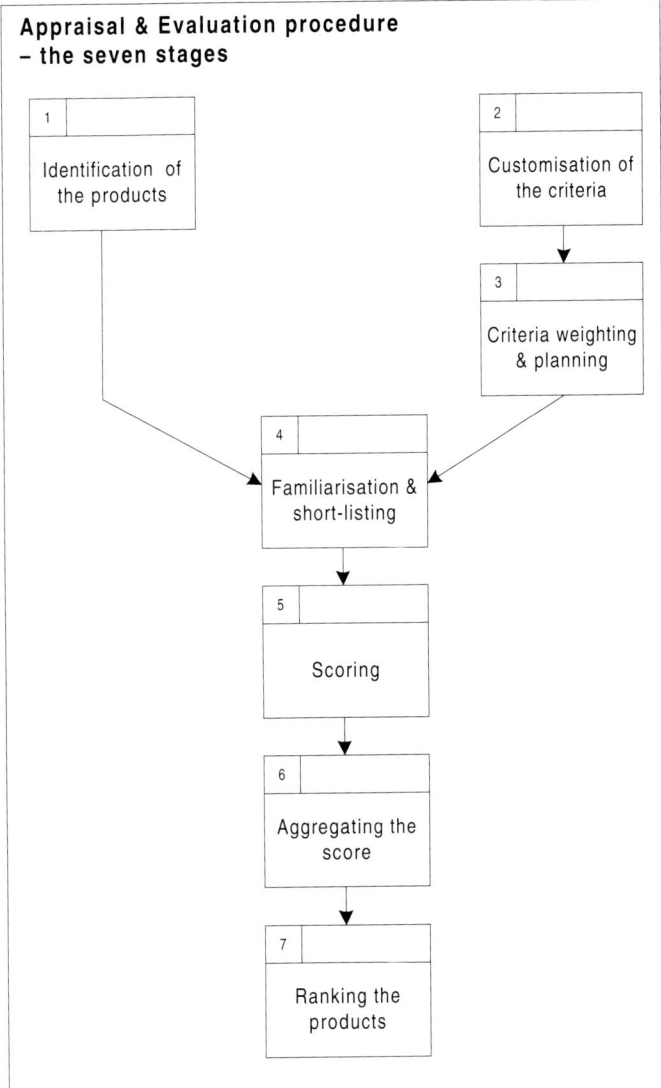

Figure 1: Appraisal & Evaluation stages

2 Scope

This volume provides clear guidelines for the appraisal and evaluation of tools to underpin *the Service Delivery Set* of the IT Infrastructure Library.

Although the evaluation criteria can form the basis of an appraisal for a custom software design they are targeted primarily at packaged software products. An evaluation can provide an assessment of the conformity between the tool's actual and desired capability or functionality. It should be noted, however, that few, if any, tools currently meet all the requirements set out in this volume and there may be organisation-specific requirements which override some of the guidelines proposed. Each organisation must prioritise its needs and decide which tool, or tools, best meet them. The guidelines provided within this volume can similarly be used by tool developers and offer a useful input to product design.

2.1 Service delivery definition

The CCTA *Service Delivery Set* of the IT Infrastructure Library provides guidelines for the management of the key delivery functions of service level management, cost management for IT services, contingency planning, capacity management and availability management.

2.2 Service delivery tools

Throughout this volume reference is made to the 'tool', meaning a comprehensive integrated tool capable of supporting all the service delivery disciplines. Ideally, service delivery tools should fully integrate with service support tools and a Configuration Management Database (CMDB) in order to allow overall centralised control of service management. Figure 2 gives a graphical representation of such an integrated product.

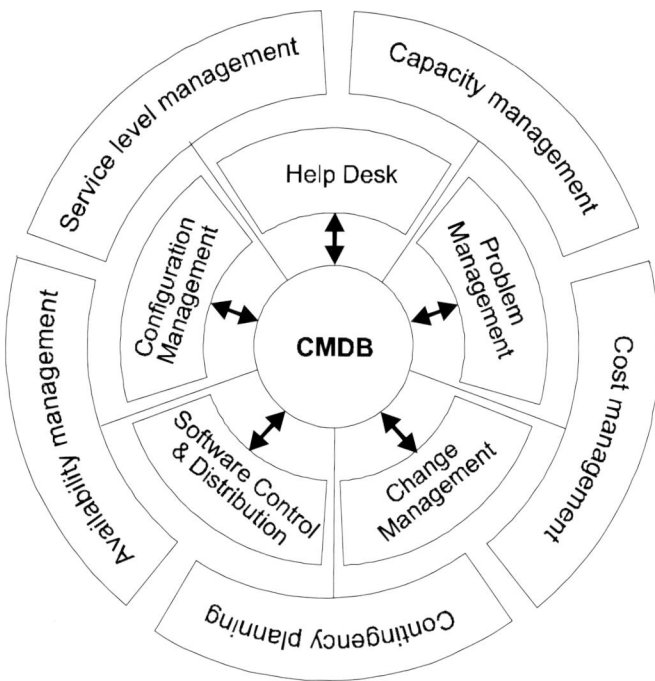

Figure 2: Integrated support tool

However, at the time of writing, there is no known product that addresses the required functionality of all five service delivery disciplines within a single tool, let alone one that also integrates support for service support.

The majority of service delivery products currently available address a single discipline, although there are some monitoring products capable of providing monitored data that will be of wider use (eg for service level management, capacity, cost and availability management purposes).

There are a growing number of emerging products which integrate the service support tools, but which do not yet incorporate much in the way of support for service delivery functionality.

Figure 2 represents an ideal which, in the longer term, it is hoped suppliers will work towards. It is recognised, however, that to achieve the functionality of such a tool in the shorter term will, at best, involve the need for a 'tool set' from a single supplier, or more likely, a 'tool box' with individual components from a number of specialist suppliers. The question of interfaces between tools from different suppliers is therefore likely to be a significant issue.

2.3 Terminology

Throughout this volume the word *organisation* is used to indicate the department or company that is purchasing the tool.

The word *user* indicates the user of the tool. At present this person is likely to work in IT infrastructure management, but it is increasingly likely that end-users will also have direct access to infrastructure management tools.

The term *end-user* indicates to a user of the IT services that the tool is intended to support such as a business user or an applications developer – a customer or 'demand side' person.

The technical IT service management terms used in this volume are explained in the IT Infrastructure Library and are, therefore, not repeated here.

3 Criteria

3.1 Notation

The criteria in this volume are structured as a hierarchy, as shown in Annex A.

The main body of the text falls into three classes:

- the main discussion of the criteria – it is primarily this text that should be customised for particular projects against which weights can be assigned and scores allotted. To obtain an overview of the criteria read the text that appears alongside a numbered heading in bold type. Where the criteria cover a large subject area they are divided into sub-criteria and appear alongside an unnumbered side heading

- detailed discussion of the criteria or sub-criteria – this level is required for information gathering

- the supporting questions associated with the criteria or sub-criteria – these are in italics.

3.2 Summary of the criteria

The hierarchy of evaluation criteria against which service delivery tools can be scored is summarised below and a diagrammatic representation of the hierarchy adopted in this volume appears at Annex A. The first four criteria are described in more detail in Chapters 4 to 7 in this volume; the remaining eight criteria are covered in Chapters 4 to 11 in the companion volume *IT Infrastructure Support Tools*. It will be necessary, of course, to construct a hierarchy applicable to the needs of any particular project or organisation, which will more than likely be a variant of the one illustrated in Annex A.

The top level criteria are:

- conformity with the IT Infrastructure Library *Service Delivery Set*

- monitoring – the ability of the tool to accept monitored data from a variety of environments

- data structure and handling – the capability of the tool's data structure to support the required functionality

- integration with other products

- openness – conformity to European, International and *de facto* standards

- usability – the quality of the user interface

- service levels for the tool – performance and availability

- backup and recovery/restart – the ability to recover from failures

- control and security – control of access and security of data

- supplier and product credibility

- costs – assessment of direct and ancillary costs of hardware, software, maintenance and people

- organisation-specific requirements and constraints.

3.3 Questions

Questions relating to the first four of the above criteria are found in the main body of this volume. Questions relating to the remaining eight criteria are covered in Chapters 4 to 11 in the companion volume *IT Infrastructure Support Tools*.

The questions should be used for familiarisation with a product before attempting to allocate scores against evaluation criteria. Not all questions are relevant to all products, or projects, and they should be used selectively.

Experience has shown that little will be gained by having the vendor provide written answers to the questions. There is the risk of different interpretations of questions or the provision of vague answers such as 'it is expected that the next revision will do that'. Only by probing can the evaluation team fully elicit the limits of the capabilities of the products. The best value will be obtained by attempting to answer questions after inspection of technical documentation and attending demonstrations.

Part 2
The Evaluation Criteria

4 Conformity with the IT Infrastructure Library

When evaluating service delivery tools for conformity with the guidance contained in the IT Infrastructure Library, the prime areas to be considered are support for the functional requirements and the level of interaction with other IT Infrastructure Library modules (and, therefore, the tools in those areas).

This section outlines the key functional requirements for each product in the service delivery support tool set. The individual IT Infrastructure Library modules should be consulted for further details.

The '80/20' rule proposes that a tool is fit for its intended purpose if it meets 80 per cent of the stated requirements (these should be based on the requirements presented in this guide and the IT Infrastructure Library). It is general practice, within Government, to divide an Operational Requirement (OR) into mandatory and desirable requirements. (It is good practice for non-government organisations to produce an OR in a similar way.) Products to be procured must meet all the mandatory requirements; ie if the 80/20 rule is applied the 20 per cent requirements not provided by the tool must be desirable requirements. This may cause a package to be rejected even though it has a good functional fit in all areas apart from one that is crucial. Therefore, when specifying the requirements try, as far as possible, to anticipate the extent to which tools are available which are capable of meeting the totality of the functionality required and make a judgement of the boundaries between mandatory and desirable requirements accordingly.

There are, of course, exceptions to the 80/20 rule, eg when no packages are capable of meeting 80 per cent of requirements. In these cases it may be necessary to select a package because of its functional design, and accept that some components must be rewritten to meet the organisation's technical requirements. However, this approach brings with it a higher degree of risk and negates some of the benefits of purchasing packaged applications.

Code modification should be avoided wherever possible. Such modifications can release the vendor from all responsibilities to support the system, and new releases or enhancements may be impossible to implement if they conflict with the modified code. Organisations that modify applications may also find that they cannot take full advantage of vendor-supplied training courses and materials. To facilitate the development of additional functionality, the application may provide interfaces or 'hooks' which can be used for both on-line and off-line 'add-ons', but care should be taken to ensure that such interfaces are 'solid' and will not be removed at future releases.

Are all mandatory requirements met?

Does the application meet at least 80 per cent of the functional requirements (mandatory and desirable) as stated in the OR?

4.1 Service level management

A comprehensive tool should support all stages in the production and ongoing management of Service Level Agreements (SLAs). SLAs may be internal (non-legally binding) agreements within an organisation, or may be part of a contractual arrangement with a third party for the provision of agreed levels of service.

SLA definition

The tool should either incorporate word processing facilities, or should have direct and easy to use interfaces with separate word processing packages, so that SLAs can be defined and developed as negotiations with users progress. An initial 'skeleton' SLA format should be offered, to enable the user to develop new SLAs quickly, with a selection of 'standard sections' that can be used as a starting point. Version control of SLAs must be maintained, and 'agreed' SLAs should be 'frozen' to prevent changes being made after this point. The IT Infrastructure Library SLA format should be offered as a default, to form the basis from which organisations may wish to progress. Sufficient flexibility is needed to meet individual needs.

Does the tool incorporate, or have close interfaces with, word processing capabilities?

Does the tool provide a skeleton SLA and 'standard sections'?

Is the tool flexible enough to meet individual needs?

SLA modelling

To establish whether proposed initial service targets are achievable (eg availability, response times, throughput),

Chapter 4
Conformity with the IT Infrastructure Library

or to assess whether an SLA target is still valid after a threshold is exceeded, the use of modelling techniques will be useful and potentially time saving. Modelling should be possible to make these assessments without having to make changes to the IT infrastructure, and risking potential adverse impact. The tool should therefore integrate with, or provide close interfaces to, modelling package(s). Please refer to sections 4.4 and 4.5 respectively, regarding similar modelling requirements for capacity and availability management.

Does the tool have an integrated modelling capability or provide close interfaces to external modelling package(s)?

SLA monitoring	Monitoring facilities will be required both before and after SLAs are agreed. Prior to agreement, service achievements must be known so that realistic targets can be incorporated in draft SLAs. After SLAs are agreed and become 'live', monitoring is needed to see whether targets have been met and to enable reporting of failures and instigation of actions in order to comply with agreements.
	Chapter 5 describes the overall monitoring requirements for all of the service delivery disciplines.
Error diagnosis and correction	The tool should allow thresholds to be set against key performance targets for reporting purposes. These thresholds should encompass sufficient margins to allow actions to be taken before a target is breached.
	Where service level thresholds are exceeded, the tool should ideally be capable of diagnosing the underlying cause and, where possible, taking predefined automated action to resolve the situation before SLA targets are breached. Where automated resolution is not possible the tool should provide all known diagnostic information to allow manual resolution.
	Is it possible to set thresholds against service achievements?
	What degree of automated error diagnosis and resolution is possible?
	What level and content of diagnostic information can be provided to assist manual resolution?
Reporting	Exception reports should be produced whenever a threshold or target is reached. Reports should be succinct and easy to understand.

Periodic reports of actual achievements should be easy to define and then automatically produced to the predefined criteria (eg content, regularity, format). Reporting facilities should be capable of aggregating data from a variety of sources to present a co-ordinated picture of service levels for each service. Easy to understand, graphical representation should be used to summarise achievements and compare these with targets. It should be possible to tailor reports to the target audience (eg IT Director, IT service manager, customers). Any trends or exceptional conditions should be capable of being highlighted.

Does the tool provide adequate exception and periodic reporting facilities?

Is it capable of aggregating data from many sources to give a co-ordinated picture?

Does the tool support the production of graphical summaries including highlighting breaches of thresholds?

Is it possible to tailor reports to specific audiences?

4.2 Cost management for IT services

The support tool should support both the costing and charging elements of cost management.

4.2.1 Costing

The tool should either provide integrated spreadsheet capabilities to allow forward IT budget estimates to be produced (based upon previous estimates where relevant) and managed, or allow interfaces to external spreadsheet products. For example, it is possible to use DDE (Direct Data Exchange) and OLE (Object Linking Environment) to pass data from a tool to a standard spreadsheet.

Careful consideration should be given to retention periods. For example, within government, in order to comply with Public Expenditure Survey (PES) estimates, the tool should allow the retention of estimates and expenditure details covering:

- the last 5 years
- the current year
- the next 3 years.

The organisation should ensure that the spreadsheet has sufficient capacity (numbers of tables, rows, columns) and accuracy (number of decimal places, significant figures) to meet its needs.

Does the tool provide integrated spreadsheet capabilities to allow budget estimates and actual expenditure to be captured and managed?

Does the spreadsheet provide sufficient capacity and accuracy for the organisation's needs?

The tool should allow spreadsheet capture of information relating to invoices received and payments made, in order to allow comparison of 'actuals' against estimates, and for estimates to be adjusted where necessary.

Ideally the tool should interface to invoice payment systems in use to allow data about actual expenditure to be captured automatically, without the need to re-enter the data.

The tool should allow classification of all costs into capital or revenue expenditure and then further sub-classification by cost units, for example:

- equipment
- software
- communications
- organisation
- accommodation.

Is there an interface to invoice payment systems to capture actual expenditure data automatically?

The tool should incorporate facilities for data entry and data storage in differing international currencies with the ability for automatic currency conversion when required.

Does the tool allow different currency data entry, storage and automatic conversion?

Where applications software is capable of providing data on the numbers of business transactions handled, the tool should be capable of accessing and using this information for cost management purposes.

Where relevant, can the tool interface to applications software to obtain business transaction data?

Data may be presented in differing formats (eg one application may record seconds and another may record milliseconds). The tool must be capable of normalising such data.

Is the tool able to normalise data arriving from applications in differing formats?

To provide adequate control of assets the tool should provide close interfaces to a Configuration Management Database (CMDB), where the location and custodian of all assets will be recorded.

Does the tool provide a close interface to a configuration management database?

All capital assets will be subject to depreciation and the tool must be capable of dealing with this effectively. Ideally this should be an automated function, working from predefined dates and optional depreciation formula criteria (eg straight line, percentage, treasury model), held in the CMDB.

The CMDB should record the capital cost of configuration items (CIs) where appropriate. This will enable an audit trail to be formed from original cost through the hierarchy of depreciation. It should be possible to retain the historical information necessary to perform the necessary calculations (eg the conversion rates at the time of original purchase).

What degree of automated support does the tool provide for dealing with depreciation?

4.2.2 Charging

The support tool requirements may vary from organisation to organisation depending upon the charging policy and methods used. In order to provide fullest flexibility the support tool should be capable of supporting a full range of charging options (see the IT Infrastructure Library module *Cost Management for IT Services* for fuller details of charging options). It should also allow for differential charging (ie reduced charges during off-peak periods, or for different users).

Does the tool support a full range of charging options and allow for differential charging using user defined algorithms?

Financial modelling	To assist an IT organisation when preparing budgets to estimate the likely outturn of a particular charging policy, a simple-to-use financial modelling capability should be provided. By defining the overall pricing method being used (eg break-even, cost plus profit margin), the charging policies and expected demand and usage figures, it should be possible to calculate the outturn at year (or period) end. *What degree of financial modelling does the tool provide to calculate expected outturn?*
Equipment held	Many charging policies will include some form of fixed or standard charge for items of equipment held by a particular customer, or group of customers (eg for each terminal, PC or printer). Charges might also be made for network connectivity. The tool must therefore enable a complete historical record to be kept of all the equipment held and all network connectivity for individual customers and/or groups of customers (to reflect the charging hierarchy) at all times during the financial period in question. This will require a close interface to the CMDB so that additions and changes can be detected and taken into account for charging purposes. *Does the tool enable a complete and up-to-date picture of equipment held and network connectivity to be maintained and used for charging purposes?*
Resource usage	Most charging policies will also include charges made for actual computing resources used by individual services (eg CPU seconds, I/Os, disc transfers, batch jobs processed, data transmission on a network). The tool should therefore provide integrated, centralised monitoring capabilities, on a per-service basis, down to individual transaction level, across a wide range of technical environments. Chapter 5 describes the overall monitoring requirements for all service delivery tools.
Charging by business transactions	The problem with raw monitored resource usage data is that it is often meaningless to the customer who is then unable to see how the charges have been derived. For this reason many organisations may choose to base some of the charges made on business transactions

processed (eg production of a payroll slip, a change of name or address on a database, an order processing transaction). Ideally the tool should automate much of this process by allowing calculation of prices per business transaction from predefined criteria and monitoring of the number of transactions of each type processed, and thus the total charges for business transactions per customer, or group of customers during a particular period.

Does the tool allow automated calculation of prices, and total charges based on monitored data, for business transactions?

Apportioning

As part of an overall charging policy, it may be necessary to apportion some shared items or services amongst a number of users (eg backup of a corporate database shared by all customers). The tool should support this by allowing apportionment to be automatically made in accordance with a predefined ratio or formula.

Does the tool allow automatic apportionment in accordance with a predefined ratio or formula?

Effort recording

Many charging systems will incorporate direct or apportioned charges for staff time. In order to determine and price the amount of time spent on supporting or providing services to individual customers or groups of customers the tool must incorporate or interface closely with a time recording system capable of recording time spent on separate tasks. It should also allow day rates to be defined and for total staff prices to be calculated for inclusion in overall charges.

Does the tool allow staff time recording and calculation of charges to be made for staff time?

Credit payments

Some charging policies may include provision for credit payments to be made for periods when agreed service targets are not met, or when specific incidents occur which breach the agreement (eg late delivery of printed output). To accommodate this the tool should be integrated with, or have close interfaces to, service level monitoring so that such breaches can be detected and the necessary credits given.

Does the tool allow monitoring of SLA breaches to enable credit payments to be calculated and made?

| | Billing | The tool should provide full support for the billing aspects of cost management. It should allow for the calculation and production of itemised statements for individual customers and/or groups of customers in accordance with a predefined charging policy (the basis on which charges will be levied) and charging structure (the individuals or groups who will be charged) and for the production of all itemised invoices, reminders, and credit notes, and processing of payments. |

Does the tool calculate and produce itemised statements, invoices, reminders and credit notes for the appropriate people or groups?

Accounting — For those organisations who need to keep separate detailed accounts of their IT income and expenditure, eg where an IT division is run as a separate business entity, the tool should provide an accounting spreadsheet capable of supporting double entry bookkeeping and to allow production of a balance sheet and profit/loss accounts.

Does the tool incorporate an accounting spreadsheet capable of supporting double entry bookkeeping and to allow production of a balance sheet and profit/loss accounts?

4.3 Contingency planning

The tool should provide full support for all aspects of business continuity planning: business impact analysis; risk analysis and management; resilience analysis and management; production and testing (and where necessary, implementation) of a business-wide contingency plan.

Link to the Capacity Management Database (CMDB) — For many of the contingency planning activities a link to an integrated CMDB, or failing that some other form of suitable inventory, will be of great value. The tool should therefore provide such a link. It should be possible to identify from the CMDB all the services provided, and the customers for those services. This will assist in deciding who to contact with questionnaires and for interviews during the Business Impact Analysis exercise.

During both risk and resilience analysis the CMDB should show the key components of the IT infrastructure and the relationships and dependencies between them. This will be invaluable when performing

Component Failure Impact Analysis (CFIA) or similar resilience analysis.

Should a disaster occur, information in the CMDB will be needed to determine the extent of the damage, both from the point of impact (which customers are affected and how?) and for replacement of equipment (what was in the fire-damaged room and who supplied it so that it can be replaced quickly?)

Note that the CMDB must be regularly backed up for contingency purposes (see Chapter 7 in the companion volume *IT Infrastructure Support Tools* for further details).

Does the tool provide a link to an integrated CMDB, or failing that some form of suitable inventory, to assist in business impact, risk and resilience analysis?

Media management

It will be essential at all times to have a complete and up-to-date record of all backup security copies, and where they are located (remote storage of security copies will be essential). Automated instigation of security copies in accordance with a predefined schedule should be possible. The tool should therefore include a media management system capable of achieving these aims, or have a close interface to an external media management system to achieve the same objectives.

Does the tool include, or provide an interface to, a media management system capable of maintaining a complete and up-to-date record of all backup security copies and their locations?

Some organisations may choose to transmit backup security copies via telecommunication links direct to off-site storage locations. The tool should support this capability and allow for acknowledgements to be returned to the home site to confirm that the copies have been successfully received.

Does the tool support transmission of security copies direct to remote locations, with acknowledgement capabilities?

It should be possible to perform periodic audits to determine if all data and media are held as expected. The tool should support this task by providing checklists of security copies and their expected

	locations. This will be particularly useful prior to testing the contingency plan, but should be regularly undertaken to guard against difficulties should a disaster occur.
	Does the tool support periodic audits to determine if all data and media are held as expected?
Risk management	The tool should support risk analysis and management. It should either include a diagnostic dialogue such that from information entered the tool should identify and prioritise risks and propose countermeasures, or have an interface to a separate tool with such capabilities. The CCTA recommended product in this area is the CCTA Risk Analysis and Management Method (CRAMM). The tool should either provide an interface to CRAMM, or should integrate or provide an interface to a comparable product offering at least equal functionality.
	Does the tool provide an interface to CRAMM or some equivalent risk analysis and management product?
Plan production	The tool should provide word processing and graphical facilities to allow a Contingency Plan to be developed and maintained. A skeleton Contingency Plan, incorporating the CCTA *proforma*, but covering full business continuity planning should be offered, with a variety of 'standard sections' available as an initial starting point. Version control is also required.
	The Contingency Plan must be placed under software control and distribution and configuration (and hence change) control to ensure that it is properly controlled and kept up to date. The CMDB should hold an up-to-date record of where each copy of the plan is located and details of the 'owner'. This information should be readily available to the contingency planner.
	Easy access to the Definitive Software Library (DSL) and CMDB is needed to achieve these objectives.
	It should be noted that the service delivery support system should itself be included in the organisation's Business Continuity Plan.
	Does the tool include word processing and graphical facilities allowing a Contingency Plan to be quickly produced from a predefined skeleton and 'standard sections'?

		Is a complete record of the location and owner of each copy of the Contingency Plan readily available?
		Is there easy access to the DSL and CMDB?
	Testing	The tool should provide support for testing the plan. Test schedules and reminders should be included together with equipment tick lists for use during test off-loads etc.
		What support is provided for testing of the Contingency Plan?

4.4 Capacity management

Capacity Management Database (CDB)

The tool should provide the capability to store all relevant capacity management data in a single logical database – the Capacity Management Database (CDB). These data will include the following:

- summarised monitored performance and throughput data
- technical data (eg performance and throughput characteristics of hardware, networks)
- workload details and characteristics
- network connectivity and host computer configuration details
- business data (number of users, number of terminals etc)
- the results of modelling and application sizing work
- the forward Capacity Plan.

To avoid the need for duplication in a number of these areas, the CDB should form an integral part of the organisation's CMDB, so the tool should ideally allow this integration.

Does the tool include a capacity management database (CDB) and is this fully integrated to the CMDB?

Performance management

The main objectives of the performance management function are to ensure that agreed service levels are maintained (in conjunction with the service level manager) and that optimum use is made of all hardware (including networks) and software resources. The tool must, therefore, be capable of monitoring all key aspects of the IT infrastructure.

Chapter 5 covers the overall monitoring requirements for all service delivery disciplines.

The tool should ideally include expert system performance analysis capabilities to produce automatic tuning recommendations.

Does the tool incorporate expert system performance analysis and automated tuning recommendations?

Workload management	A primary role of workload management is to understand and document all workloads and their characteristics (eg what type of workload – transaction processing, batch, print; what level of resource usage; frequency). The tool should allow these details to be held as part of the CDB (ideally as an integral part of the CMDB).

The initial task of identifying workloads will be made easier if full access is available to the CMDB to identify the services offered (a workload will normally equate to all, or a discrete part, of a service) and the customers of that service. Additionally, it is easier to perform workload forecasting if estimated throughput figures from agreed SLAs are also available. Ideally these should be held as a part of the CMDB so the tool should allow ready access to the CMDB for these purposes.

Does the tool allow workload details and characteristics to be held as part of the CDB (ideally as an integral part of the CMDB)?

Is ready access to service and customer information on the CMDB available to allow initial identification of workloads?

To identify resource usage characteristics of individual workloads it will be necessary to have ready access to the monitored performance data mentioned in Chapter 5.

Does the tool allow ready access to monitored performance data for workload management purposes?

Resource management	One of the responsibilities of resource management is to establish and manage a data storage management system. The tool should therefore either include facilities to achieve this or have close interfaces to external

systems with this functionality. The tool should allow disc layouts to be planned in advance and incorporate modelling capabilities to enable 'what if' questions to be asked and answered without having to implement any proposed changes into the live environment which might have adverse impact upon user services (eg what would be the likely effect if we move File A from Disc 001 to Disc 002?).

Does the tool incorporate or have interfaces to facilities for planning and modelling data storage and in particular disc layouts?

Modelling

The ability to predict the behaviour of a computer or network system and the ability to assess SLA targets under a given volume or variety of work is a fundamental requirement of capacity management. Monitoring of previous traffic and performance will give a good indication of likely behaviour, but there will be cases where monitored data is either not available (eg new systems) or not valid (eg where significant changes have been made to an existing system). The tool must therefore incorporate easy-to-use modelling capabilities to allow the prediction of likely device and network utilisation levels, online response times, batch turn round times and disc space (as mentioned earlier).

The tool should have in-built, or access to, information on the performance and throughput characteristics of all equipment and network types in use, or of potential use, to be used for modelling purposes. Ideally it should not be necessary to store this information separately. It should be accessible from the CDB, which should be an integral part of the CMDB.

The results of modelling must be easy to calibrate against actual performance data. There should therefore be an automated link to monitored performance data (see Chapter 5) and amendments to the model to achieve this calibration should be easy and quick to make.

The tool should have comprehensive reporting facilities providing workload summaries, eg of total utilisations and response times, and workload detail, eg breakdown of response times by device.

Does the tool incorporate easy to use modelling capabilities and have access to device and network performance and throughput criteria, ideally via the CMDB?

Is there an automated link to monitored performance data and is it possible to calibrate and amend models easily and quickly?

Does the tool have comprehensive reporting facilities?

Application sizing

The primary objective of sizing is to estimate the hardware resources that are necessary to support a proposed application and provide the required service levels. Although it is possible, providing the necessary information is available, to size new applications by mathematical calculations on paper, this is very time consuming and should not be necessary. Specialist modelling capabilities should therefore be provided to allow application sizing to be performed automatically. These capabilities should include the ability to cater for a range of transaction frequencies per business function, and a range of possible database accesses per business function within a single model.

The application development lifecycle should be under configuration management control (ideally utilising the same integrated CMDB as used for configuration management of the live IT infrastructure). The tool should provide automated interfaces so that, as applications are designed and developed, whenever new information about the proposed application becomes available this can trigger off further sizing work to incorporate the new information. As applications software becomes available and details are recorded in the CMDB, this should trigger a similar reaction.

The accuracy of application sizing will be dependent upon the accuracy of any business information on which it is based (number of users, transaction rates, peaks etc). To achieve maximum accuracy the tool should provide easy access to such business data, ideally via the CMDB.

Does the tool provide specialist modelling capabilities to allow sizing of new applications?

Are there links with the application lifecycle, ideally via the CMDB, which trigger the need for further sizing work?

Is easy access provided to business information held in the CMDB?

Demand management	Normally it will be preferable to manage demand through incentives (eg reduced costs for work processed off-peak, see section 4.2) but there may be critical circumstances when demand has to be reduced via restrictions (eg limiting or reducing the number of concurrent users to preserve the quality of service to those users who are allowed to process work). On such occasions the capacity manager will need ready access to work scheduling software and/or transaction processing software to implement any such restrictions. The tool should provide this easy access.

Does the tool provide easy access to work scheduling software to allow implementation of any required restrictions? |
| Capacity Plan | The tool should incorporate word processing and graphics capabilities to allow the written Capacity Plan to be drafted and developed. Ideally a 'skeleton' plan should be offered which can be used as a starting point. To ensure that the plan is properly controlled and kept up to date, the plan should be placed under software control and distribution and configuration (and hence change) control. The tool should therefore allow easy access to the Definitive Software Library (DSL) and CMDB to achieve this.

Does the tool incorporate word processing facilities and include a 'skeleton' Capacity Plan?

Is there easy access to the DSL and CMDB? |

4.5 Availability management

Availability monitoring	The tool must allow monitoring of the availability levels of each service, as perceived by the customers (monitoring requirements for the whole of service delivery are covered in Chapter 5). The tool should allow downtime data to be gathered, affected services to be identified, and reports to be generated.

Does the tool allow service availability, as perceived by the customers, to be monitored?

The tool should make it possible, by reference to the help desk log and CMDB, to identify those incidents affecting availability that are attributable to external suppliers such as maintainers and providers of outsourced services, so that claims for service credits can be made against them.

Does the tool allow incidents caused by third parties to be identified?

Availability modelling

A major responsibility of availability management (in conjunction with contingency planning) is to ensure that the IT infrastructure is as resilient to failure as affordably possible. In this way the likelihood of non-availability will be reduced.

To achieve this the availability manager needs easy access to the CMDB to be able to identify all key components and to assess vulnerabilities (through relationships and dependencies) and threats (through historical failure information). It is also helpful to have access to historical failure information to determine trends and highlight potential weaknesses.

Resilience and availability modelling is helpful, for example:

- when deciding how effective a proposed change will be
- assessing the likely impact of a new service on the availability levels of existing services
- ensuring that new services can meet their availability requirements.

The tool should provide the capability to model mathematically the likely impact if one or more components are replaced, duplicated, or otherwise amended in an attempt to improve resilience, and calculate the likely effect upon availability (and performance) levels. The model should be capable of allowing the comparison between several possible scenarios in order to identify the most cost effective option(s). In order to achieve this the model will need access to any previous history of failures and incident rates etc, and have access to SLA details. These should be readily available, ideally via the CMDB.

Does the tool incorporate resilience and availability modelling capabilities and have ready access to CMDB relationship, dependency and historical failure information?

Incident prevention

The tool should incorporate, or have close links to, event monitoring software (which may be used for automated operating purposes). All events throughout the IT infrastructure should be centrally reported for investigation and handling. It should be possible to set thresholds against likely events and to raise alerts when thresholds are exceeded (eg to detect when an area on a disc is becoming full, before it overflows and causes a failure; to identify when an off-line job has failed to start by a particular time).

Does the tool incorporate or have close links to event monitoring software?

Is it possible to set thresholds and raise alerts if these are exceeded?

The tool should have the capability of automatically assessing each event for characteristics, impact and severity.

Where it is possible for a predefined response to an event to be taken to overcome an impending failure (eg allocate further disc space for 'emergency' use) the tool should do this and report its actions to a log file for later inspection.

Can the tool assess events and perform automated preventative action where this can be predefined?

Where it is not possible to take automated preventative action the tool should take the necessary steps to call for human intervention. The specific actions taken should be capable of being defined according to the impact and severity levels. The range of options should include:

- simple logging of events to a file for later analysis
- reporting of events to a screen (to be located with support staff) with the capability to trigger flashing visual alarms and audible alarms where appropriate

- full alarm instigation – where necessary contacting support staff via paging devices etc.

Is the tool capable of calling for human intervention, offering a range of options depending upon the impact and severity of the event?

5 Monitoring

With the exception of contingency planning, all of the service delivery disciplines require that a great deal of monitoring be performed. This section covers the monitoring requirements for the whole of service delivery, to remove the need for duplication in other sections.

Much of the monitoring to be performed must be carried out on specific platforms or in specific environments. However, unless monitoring is properly controlled, there is significant scope for much duplication of effort and heavy resource overheads. Therefore, the service delivery tool should ideally be host platform independent, running on a dedicated platform and not on any of the host machines being monitored. This will allow greater resilience and ensure that the tool does not colour or degrade the performance of the operational system.

There is, therefore, a requirement, as shown in Figure 3, for the service delivery tool to incorporate a *filter* capable of accepting monitored data from a wide range of external technical environments (eg mainframe, Unix and MS DOS), normalising and storing this data within a centralised database, ideally the CMDB. This will have the effect of consolidating the data gathered and make it available to each of the service delivery disciplines without the need for duplication.

The filter should hold *data translation specification files* capable of recognising and normalising all common formats.

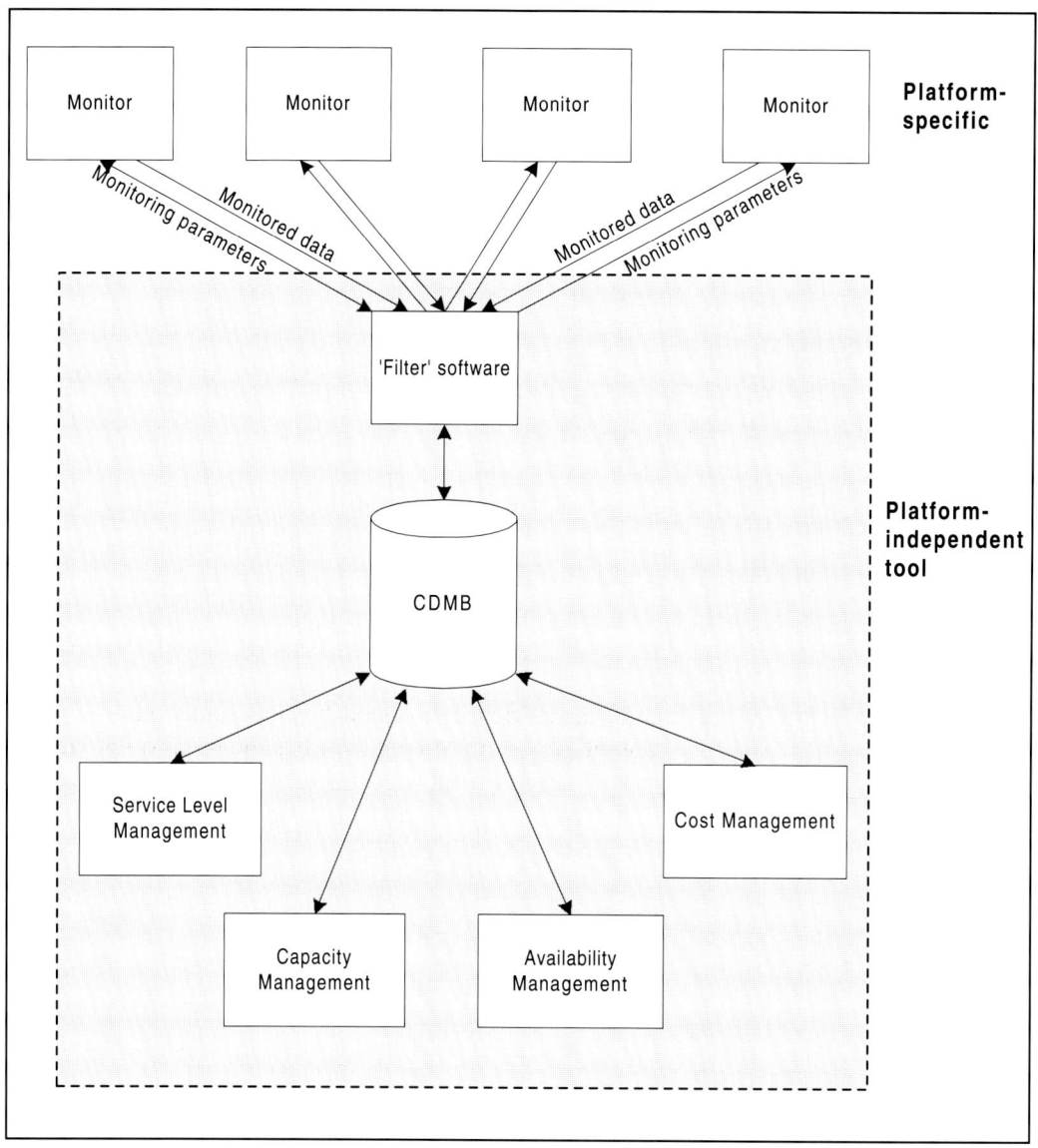

Figure 3: Monitoring requirements

Is the tool capable of gathering and filtering monitored data from all required technical environments and normalising and storing this in a centralised location where it can be used by all service delivery applications?

Does the tool run on a dedicated platform, making it independent of the environments being monitored?

As much of the monitoring on the host machines will be parameter driven, the tool should be capable of transmitting parameter details out to specific locations in order to control the frequency and format of the data to be monitored and returned to the central filter.

Is the tool capable of controlling the parameters of host monitors to manage the frequency and format of monitored data?

It should be possible to 'timetable' the level of monitoring to meet requirements. For example it may not be necessary to report poor performance at a time when the service is not guaranteed, and less frequent 'snapshots' may be needed at off-peak times.

Is it possible to 'timetable' the level of monitoring?

The level of data held should make it possible to report on individual transactions and/or transaction types with different targets for individual users.

Is it possible to report on individual transactions and/or transaction types with different targets for individual users?

In order to identify possible bottlenecks or other potential performance difficulties the monitored data should be stored and reported in such a way that trends are easily identified.

Are data stored and reported in such a way that trends are easily identified?

5.1 Monitoring details

The matrix in Figure 4 shows some examples of the various items that can be monitored, and the disciplines that will use each item of data. There is a degree of overlap on some of the items, but the purposes for which the data is used will vary. If the centralised filtering system described earlier in this section is used there should be no need for duplicated monitoring resources.

Item to be monitored	Disciplines using data
availability	SLM, AM, Cost
service downtime	SLM, AM, Cost
number of service breaks	SLM, AM, Cost
terminal response times	SLM, Cap
workload throughput	SLM, Cap
batch job run times	SLM, Cap
incident handling/resolution times	SLM, Cap
problem handling/resolution times	SLM, AM, Cost
processor utilisation	SLM, AM, Cost
memory usage	Cap, Cost
paging and swapping rates	Cap
I/O utilisation	Cap, Cost
batch job resource data (elapsed times, CPU, I/O etc)	Cap, Cost
transaction rates	SLM, Cap, Cost
transaction resource usage	Cap, Cost
network traffic data and characteristics	SLM, Cap, Cost

Key:
- AM – Availability management
- Cap – Capacity management
- Cost – Cost management
- SLM – Service level management

Figure 4: Monitoring of customer service

Is the tool capable of monitoring all the above mentioned elements?

5.2 Monitoring of customer service

A primary responsibility of the service level management and availability management functions is to determine the true customer perception of service quality. To assist in this the tool should ideally provide monitoring at the point of delivery. For availability, service breaks and response time monitoring this will require monitoring 'at the terminal'.

At the time of writing there is no known method of monitoring dumb terminals from a central point. Even where all terminals in use have intelligence, the potential overhead costs of monitoring all terminals may be excessive. To overcome this the tool should allow some form of 'sampling' to give a good indication of service achievements without excessive overheads. The tool should allow flexible definition of the terminals to be sampled to accurately reflect actual usage and hence user perception.

Does the tool allow availability, reliability, and response time monitoring 'at the terminal' for all terminals connected to the network?

If 'at the terminal' monitoring is not available for all terminals, is there a sampling capability capable of accurately assessing terminal response times?

An alternative method of gauging terminal response times, with reasonable accuracy, is to combine computer response times and network response times. To achieve this the tool must either incorporate computer and network monitors or allow close interfaces to external monitors, and provide the capability to centrally gather, analyse and report on response times across the IT infrastructure.

If 'at the terminal' monitoring, or sampling, is not available, does the tool allow close monitoring of computers and networks to measure terminal response times with reasonable accuracy?

Where no other monitoring capabilities exist, one possible method of recording service quality may be to assume that the service levels are satisfactory unless notified otherwise by the customers. Such notification must be via the help desk where details can be recorded. In such cases it will be necessary to access the help desk data. Additionally, service quality may be determined via SLA reviews where customers will, no doubt, voice any dissatisfaction with service quality. Such reactions could be recorded as incidents (via the help desk) and accessed for use in determining service quality.

Availability (or at least unavailability) can be implied from the failure of some crucial intermediate component. This is facilitated by access to the CMDB to determine the items and services affected by the critical component.

Does the tool have access to the help desk and CMDB?

Is the tool able to access performance and availability data as monitored and recorded by the help desk?

6 Data structure and handling

A major force of change affecting IT infrastructures today results from a requirement for greater integration. The tools which are used to manage the IT infrastructure must be able to accommodate changes in the criticality, size and complexity of the technology solutions that the organisation will wish to implement. Integration of multi-vendor infrastructure components and the need to absorb new components in the future, will place particular demands on the data handling and modelling capabilities of the tools. If different components of service provision are outsourced to different suppliers this could be even more of a problem in providing an integrated tool set.

Individual tools may have separate database or file structures, but ideally an integrated tool will have an integrated configuration management database at its centre. At present this is most likely to be based on some form of relational database technology that supports the ability to model highly complex data structures while providing the tool set with a degree of independence from the database structure. Regardless of the underlying technology, which may change, the capabilities of the data definition and manipulation language, together with the flexibility of the data item constructs, may have a major influence on whether a tool conforms to installation requirements.

In the long term, despite careful analysis of requirements, it is likely that there will be a need to modify the logical structure of the database. These changes may arise because of new requirements, evolution of the IT infrastructure which the tools must support and the migration to new architectural standards within the infrastructure, as these become more mature and stable.

The database design must be flexible enough to meet the future needs of the organisation. The overhead of providing for data items that may not, initially, be used, may be far less than the cost of redesigning the database. The data model is the most important component of the tool. If the data design is solid, new processes can be added at a later stage with a reduced conversion risk.

In assessing the data structure capabilities of the tool the following areas should be examined to ensure that the tool meets the current requirements of the organisation and has sufficient flexibility to continue to do so in the future without jeopardising the organisations investment:

- original data definition quality
- ability to change the data definition
- data manipulation facilities
- conformance to standards.

6.1 Data definition and data flow

In order to support the functional requirements documented in the *Service Delivery Set* of the IT Infrastructure Library, the following high level data flow diagrams (Figures 5 to 10) are proposed as examples of the required information flow. These may be useful when determining the functional boundaries of a particular tool and should provide a better understanding of the requisites by showing where data is stored, how it flows between processes, and which processes access data.

Each diagram shows which components are integral to the specific tool in question and how information provided by other components of the infrastructure management tool set will also be required. (For specific integration requirements see Chapter 7).

Figure 5 is an overview diagram that shows the integration between the key components of service delivery and the interfaces with other infrastructure management functions and business and planning functions.

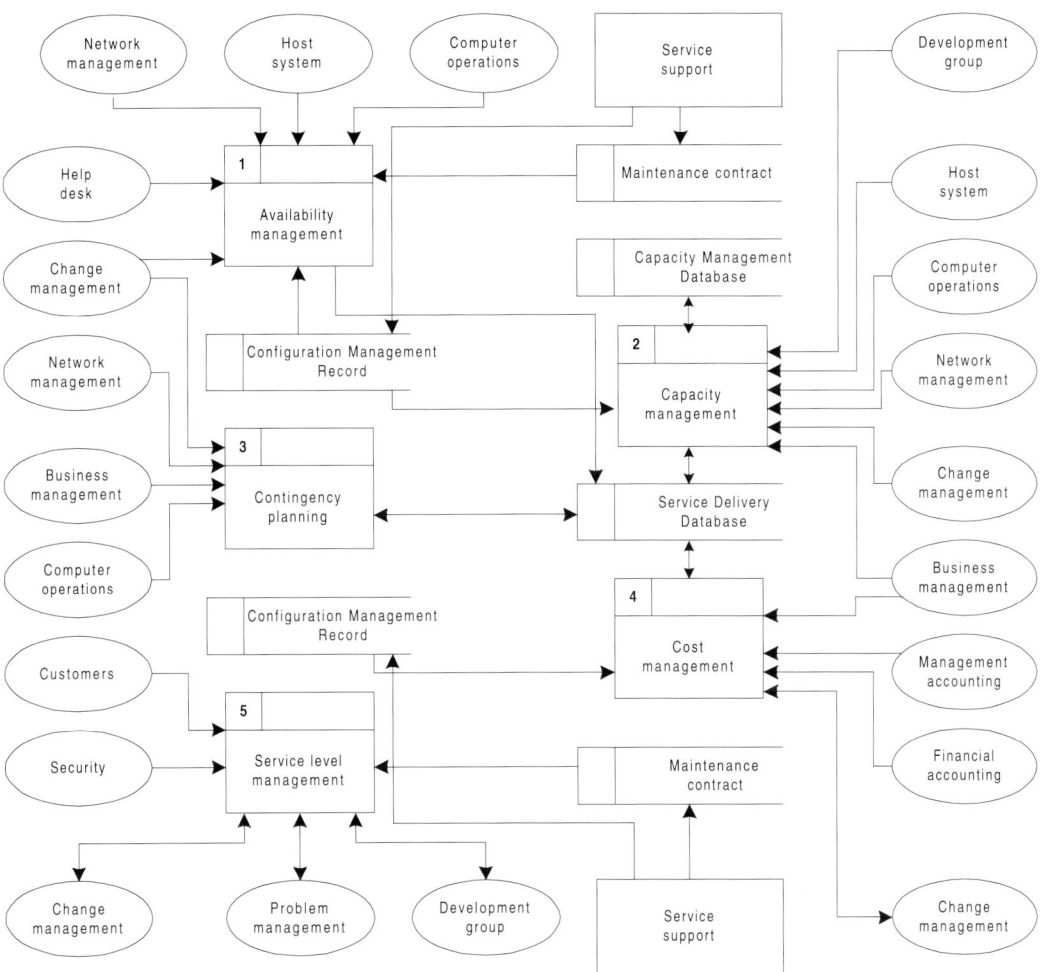

Figure 5: Service delivery overview

The service level management tool, Figure 6, should support the creation and maintenance of a service catalogue and the creation and management of Service Level Agreements (SLAs).

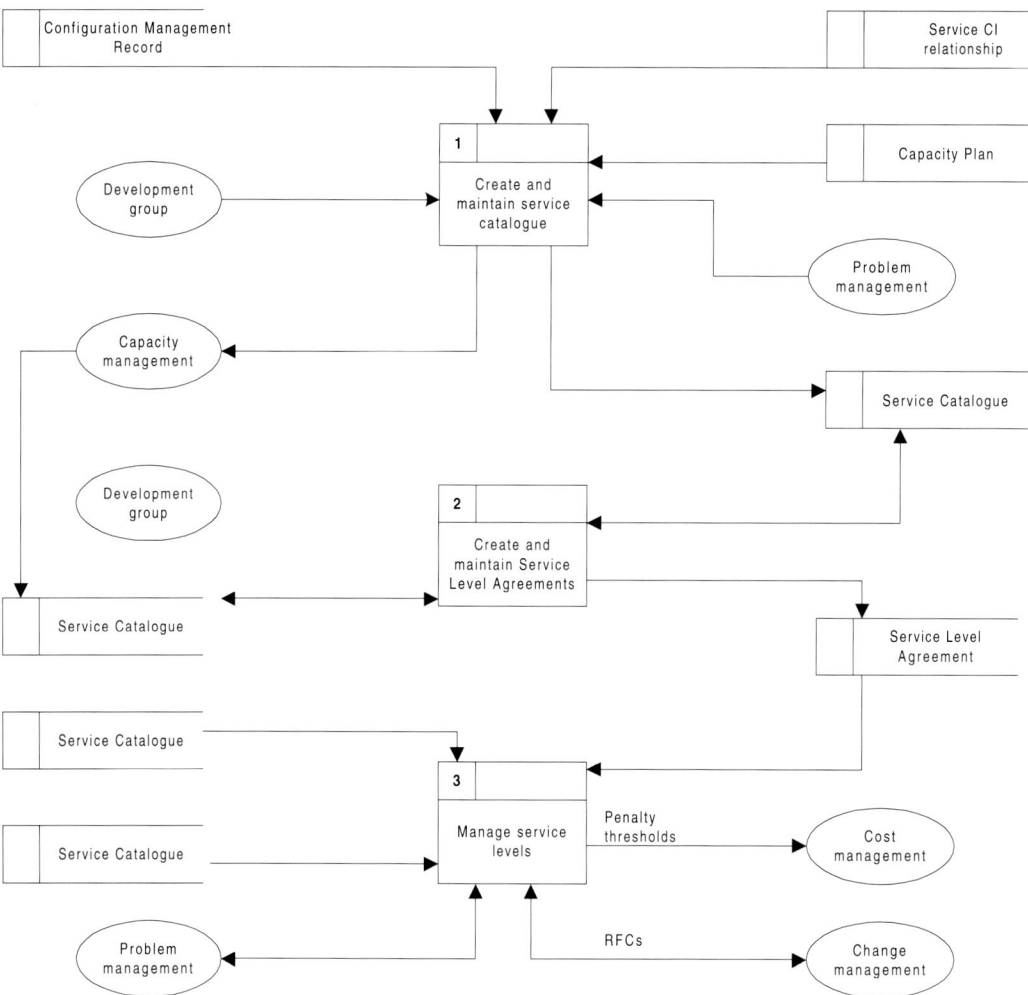

Figure 6: Service level management dataflow

Chapter 6
Data structure and handling

The cost management tool, Figure 7, should support estimating and managing costs and, where appropriate, the formulation and ongoing management of a charging policy.

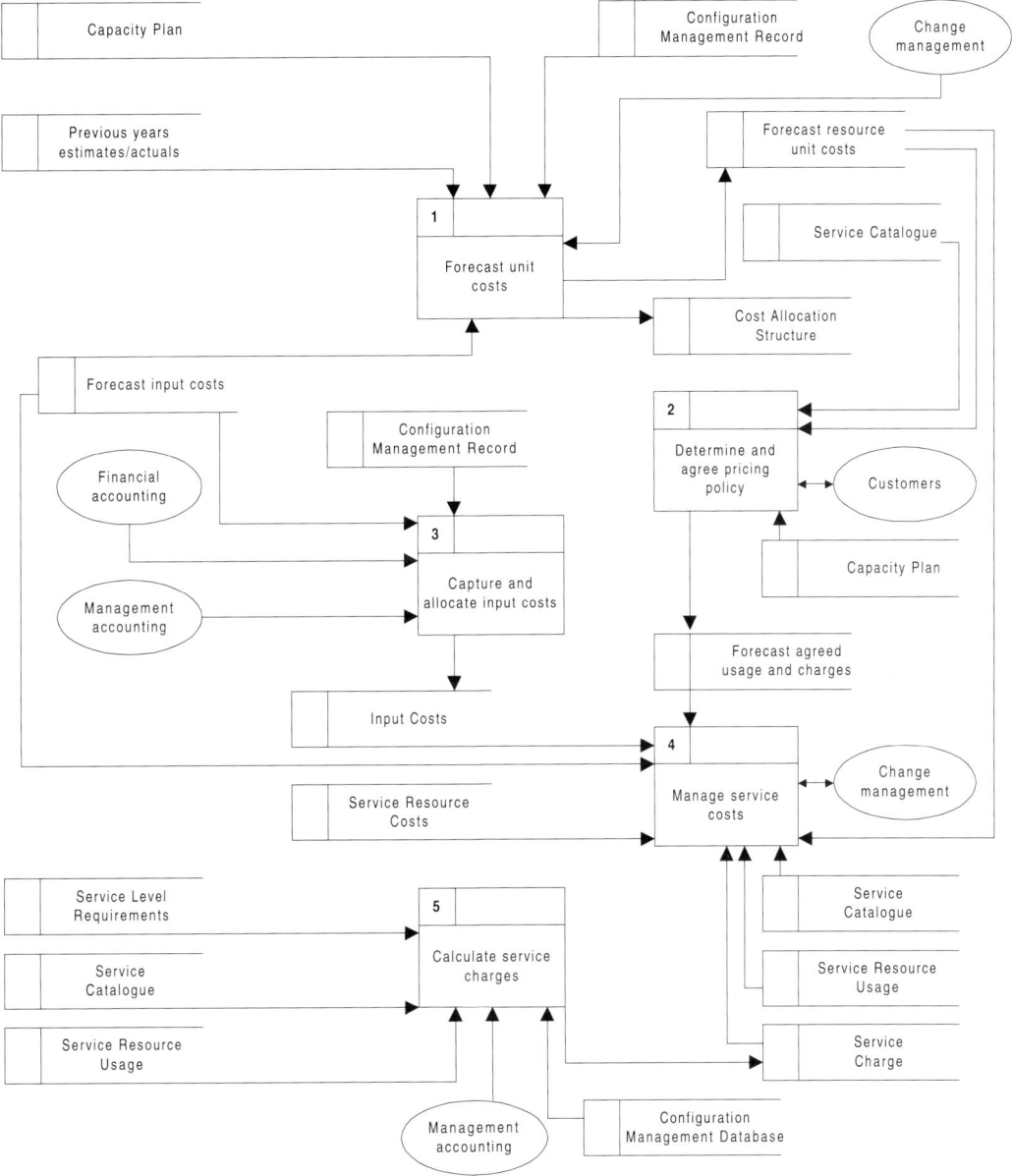

Figure 7: Cost management dataflow

The contingency planning tool, Figure 8, should support the assessment of risk and the identification and implementation of countermeasures and the creation and management of a Contingency Plan capable of providing business continuity should a disaster occur.

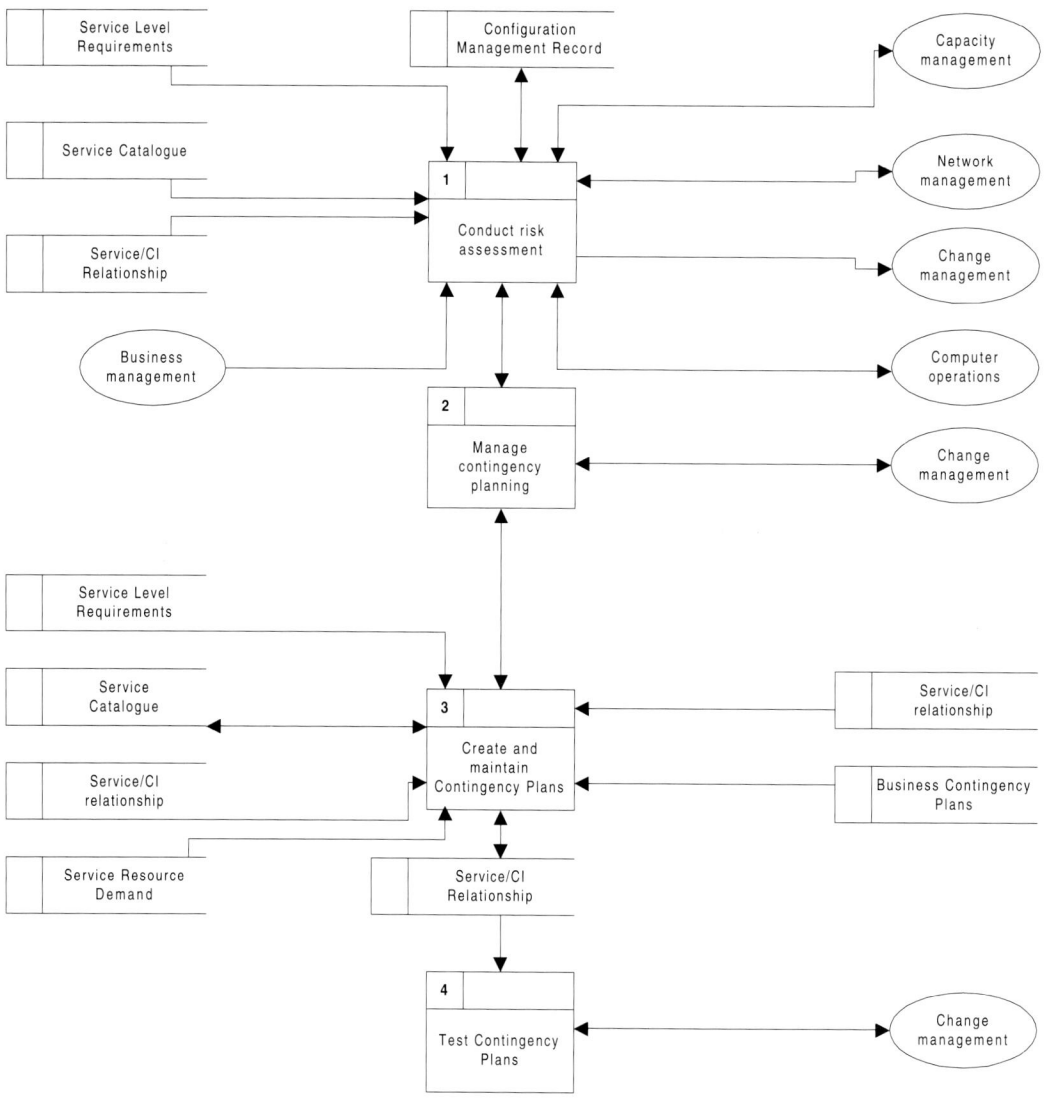

Figure 8: Contingency planning dataflow

Chapter 6
Data structure and handling

The capacity management tool, Figure 9, must provide support for workload management and performance management and for the production and maintenance of a Capacity Plan.

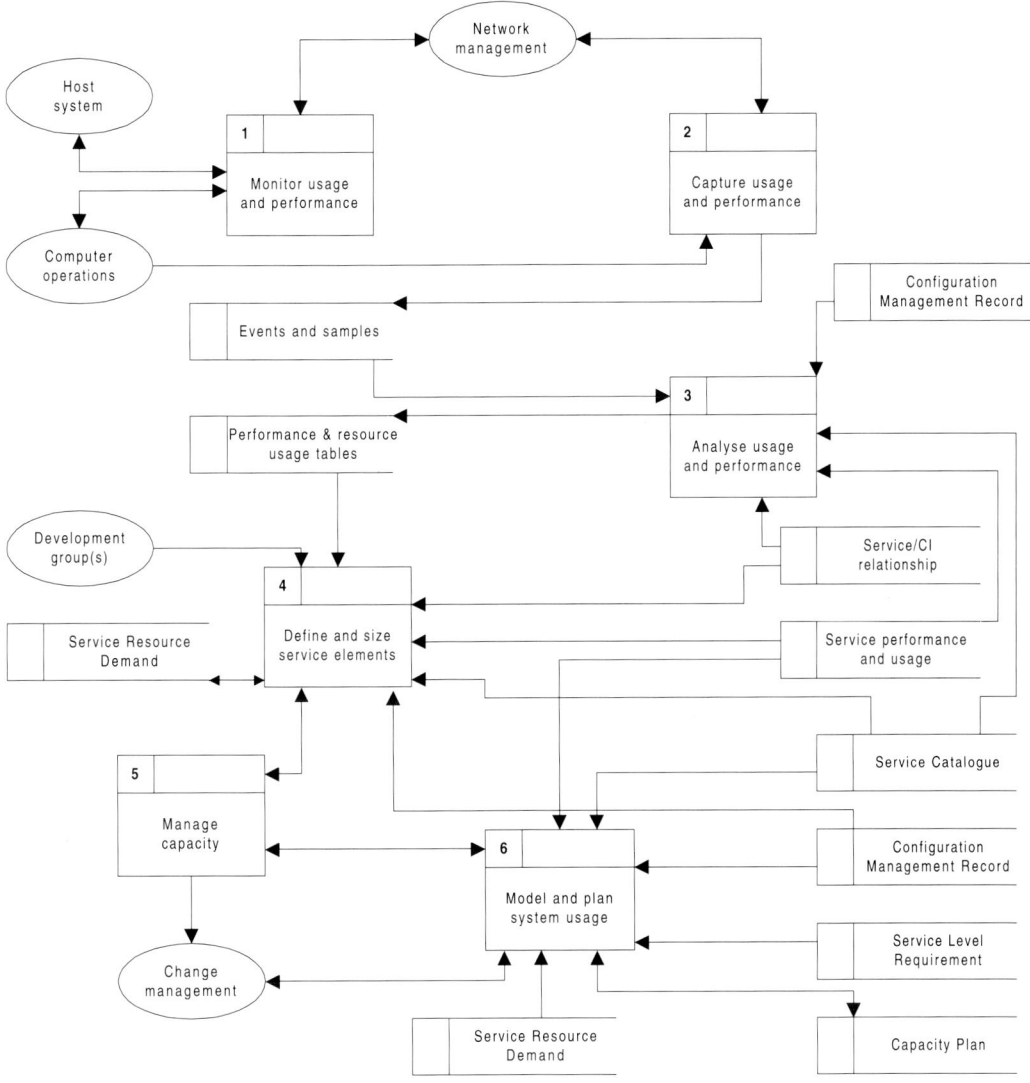

Figure 9: Capacity management dataflow

The availability management tool, Figure 10, must allow availability, serviceability and reliability levels to be forecast, monitored and managed.

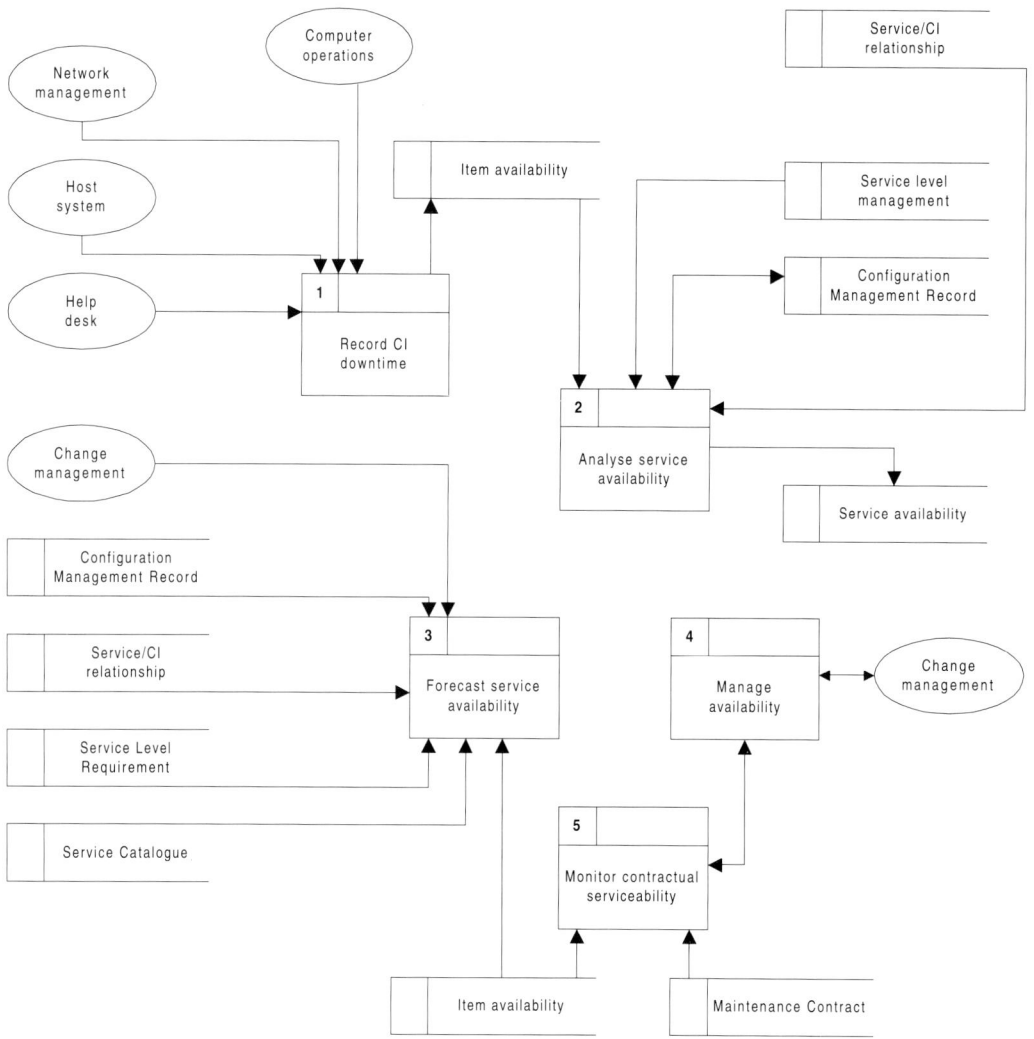

Figure 10: Availability management dataflow

Chapter 6
Data structure and handling

Logical data structure definition

To enable changes to be made to the logical data structure of a database it is important to ensure its independence from the physical database design. The latter is often dictated by performance requirements and installation characteristics.

Can logical data definitions be enhanced and modified without extensive changes to the physical database definition?

The ease with which changes can be made to the logical data structure is vital in protecting the investment the organisation makes in any particular tool.

What constraints are there in making changes to the logical data structure?

The use of logical data views, which provide access to the subset of the data held within a database and present it in a logical format which is independent of the underlying structure, will also be important in creating a level of independence between a tool and its underlying database.

The various infrastructure management applications which access the underlying database may have a requirement for data of different data types, eg decimal, binary, floating point.

Does the tools underlying database support the use of application specific views?

Data independence may also allow a database administrator to change storage structures or data access strategies, as required, with minimum impact on existing applications. This will allow new data to be added to the database, new standards to be adopted, and even new application priorities or relative performance requirements to be accommodated. Over time, different data items may need to be accessed more frequently or in different ways. It should be possible to reorganise the data to meet the changing requirements.

Is there sufficient data independence to make it possible to reorganise data as needed to meet changing requirements?

Data item definition

Support for user-defined data ranges and data types improves the flexibility of the tool. Such flexibility enhances storage and validation efficiency. It also allows

55

the organisation to tailor the data handling of the tool to its own specific requirements.

Does the tool allow the user to define data types and valid data ranges?

Data retention periods will affect the sizing requirements of the database implementation and these should be examined to determine the initial and future storage requirements. As the distribution of data values and data volumes change, different storage structures may be needed to maintain performance levels and to rationalise disk usage. This may become particularly important as the quality of historical data gathered by the help desk increases and trends in data distribution become more evident.

Does the proposed database implementation allow modification of storage structures?

The tool must be able to support unstructured data as well as the usual formats supported by most databases (numeric, alphanumeric etc). The service level management system for example must make provision for SLA details to be held as free text. The Appraisal and Evaluation Library guide to *Text-based Information Management Systems* provides further information on this topic.

Can the tool support the storage and rapid retrieval of free text?

6.2 Data definition modification

The ability of the tool to model and support an evolving infrastructure and to reflect changes within the organisation will reduce pressures for significant changes to the physical database. This is directly dependent on the quality of the data design. In cases where requirements change over time and database restructuring or reorganisation is inevitable the tool should allow changes to be made to the physical data structure with minimum disruption. See also the section on logical data structure definition (section 6.1).

The types of changes that may occur will depend on the stability of the IT infrastructure. For instance the cost management and capacity management databases may need to be reorganised as historical financial and performance data build up, if response times when accessing this data are to be maintained.

What database restructuring facilities exist?

Is it possible to add, delete and rename data items and change the relationships between record types?

What facilities exist to improve performance?

The restructuring of the database can be particularly time consuming and complex. The process may be further complicated if the database is populated by large quantities of data which must be unloaded before changes can be made. As a result the restructuring process may impact on the availability of the tool.

Can restructuring take place while the application is still running?

What utilities are available to assist restructuring?

6.3 Data manipulation

In addition to the standard data manipulation functions such as record insertion, selection, modification and deletion, the tool should support advanced user defined queries. It should be possible to create management reports based on the extraction and manipulation of statistical information, eg to provide service level management and availability statistics to show operational performance, and to create complex diagnostic and capacity planning reports based on the configuration database, while maintaining on-line response times that are acceptable to the organisation.

What user defined query functionality is supported?

6.4 Standards

Tools that conform to current relevant standards will in general accommodate changes to their data structures more readily, provide data structures that can be used by other tools and safeguard the organisations investment in skills and training.

Support for industry standards

The SQL (Structured Query Language) data definition and manipulation language is the recommended international standard for relational database products (ISO 9075:1989). The current SQL standard was defined by the American National Standards Institute (ANSI). However, most commercial database systems add proprietary extensions to this definition.

Is the database structure based on accepted standards?

What degree of conformity to this standard is supported and what, if any, proprietary additions have been made?

Support for installation standards

The proposed DBMS should be compatible with the existing DBMS implementations within the organisation and in line with the planning policy for system architecture. This will allow future systems to be integrated, skills can be made portable across systems, support costs can be reduced and investment in training is safeguarded.

Does the tools data definition and manipulation language conform to the organisations standards?

7 Integration with other products

System integration addresses the requirements of IT systems that need to exchange information and synchronise their operations. For example, both payroll and personnel systems need access to employee data.

The benefits of integration include:

- reduced data redundancy and keying
- widespread availability of accurate and up-to-date information, which will be consistent throughout the organisation
- a reduction in resource requirements in terms of hardware, software and manpower.

Integration can also vastly improve the usefulness, value, power and functionality of products. The total of all these factors for an integrated product, or set of products, can often far outweigh the sum of the component parts. In some cases extra facilities or functions can be made available through integration that did not exist in individual components.

Figure 11, overleaf, shows how multiple IT service management functions require access to common information.

Ideally the interfaces between all service management tools should be via a centralised CMDB, as shown in Figure 2, but it is recognised that, at present, some or all of these interfaces will have to be made directly between the separate products. The level of inter-operability between separately procured tools is therefore very important. Common data formats and even inter-process communication are more easily achieved if the specific tools are implemented to open systems standards.

Functions \ Data Items	Configuration item	SLA criteria	End user details	Incident	Problem/ known error	Request for change	Performance data
Service level management	R	C/U/R	U/R	R	R	U/R	R
Cost management	U/R	U/R					R
Contingency planning	R/U	R				R	R
Capacity management	C/U/R	R				R	C/U/R
Availability management	R	R		R			R
Configuration management	C/U/R		C/U/R			U/R	
Help desk	R	R	R	C/U/R	R		
Problem management	R			R	C/U/R	R	R
Change management	R	R				C/U/R	
Software control & distribution	U/R		R			U/R	
Network management	C/U/R	R		C/U/R	U/R	U/R	C/U/R
Operations management	U/R	R		C/U/R	U/R	R	

Key 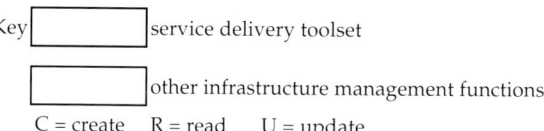 service delivery toolset

☐ other infrastructure management functions

C = create   R = read   U = update

Figure 11: Information usage by key functions

It is essential that the selected tool is interfaced with other infrastructure management tools, but the requirement for integration also extends to other systems which may be used by service delivery groups or the organisation as a whole.

A service delivery tool may also be required to interface directly with the live environment, for example to collect monitored raw performance data or resource accounting information. The nature of the integration, ie real-time or off-line, is important and is influenced by the criticality of the service delivery function. The direction of flow of information should also be considered as the tool should be able to export and import data as required.

This section examines three different aspects of the integration requirements of each of the service delivery functions:

- integration with other infrastructure support tools
- integration with other IT systems used to support business functions outside the IT service organisation

Chapter 7
Integration with other products

- integration with the live environment.

7.1 Service level management

There is a primary need for the service level management tool to interface with a range of monitoring systems to determine whether SLA targets have been met. There are also a number of interfaces needed when planning and drafting SLAs.

Interfaces with other infrastructure support tools

The service level management tool should interface with other service delivery functions, such as:

- capacity management
- availability management
- cost management
- contingency planning

and with other infrastructure management functions such as configuration management, help desk/problem management and change management.

If the service level management tool does not have integrated modelling facilities, interfaces will be necessary to capacity management modelling facilities to allow initial assessment of whether service targets are achievable and to ask 'what if' questions for diagnostic purposes or when assessing proposed changes.

If no integrated modelling exists, does the tool have an interface to capacity management modelling facilities?

In order to determine whether service targets have been met, interfaces are needed with monitoring tools supporting availability management and the performance management aspects of capacity management (see Chapter 5).

Where complete service availability measurement is not obtainable centrally, an organisation may wish to monitor the customer perception of service availability via the help desk, and will in any case wish to monitor the levels of support being provided by the help desk. The tool should therefore be either integrated with, or allow close interfaces to, help desk and problem management tools in order to readily obtain accurate data on incident and problem management handling and resolution statistics and to obtain user perception of service availability. When dealing with incidents, it will be helpful for help desk staff to know the key SLA targets and achievements for individual customers or groups of customers. The tool should, therefore, provide this information via these interfaces.

Does the tool integrate with, or allow close interfaces to, help desk and problem management tools?

Where charges are made for IT service provision, and where service targets are not met, credit payments may have to be made in accordance with agreed contractual arrangements. The service level management tool should therefore interface to cost management tool(s) to allow any required credit payments to be triggered.

Does the tool interface with cost management system(s) to allow credit payments to be triggered?

Separate SLAs or degraded service levels may be applicable in the period immediately following a major incident or disaster. The tool should therefore interface with the contingency planning details (either held on the CMDB or Service Catalogue) to determine what service levels apply.

Does the tool have interfaces to contingency planning information so that service levels following a disaster can be determined?

The service level management function must be involved in the assessment of proposed changes to determine the likely impact on existing service levels. There must therefore be an interface with the change management system to allow this, ideally as a close coupled function of complementary modules or via some form of electronic mail. Access to the CIs and relationships on the CMDB will assist in the assessment process, so an interface that allows this is also needed.

Does the tool have a direct interface with change management and the CMDB?

Interfaces with other tools being used within the organisation	For new business application systems being developed, Service Level Requirements (SLRs) must be established early in the design stage. These SLRs can be refined throughout the software development lifecycle and will eventually become SLAs. Interfaces are therefore required between the development tools (eg CASE

Chapter 7
Integration with other products

tools) and the service level management tool to allow SLR information to be exchanged.

Is there a link to tools that support the development method, such as CASE tools, to allow SLR data to be exchanged?

In cases where it is not possible to monitor directly end-user terminal response times and availability levels, it may be necessary to obtain network performance and availability information in order to estimate or calculate terminal response times. In such cases, interfaces to network management tools will be required.

If necessary, is there an interface to network management tools?

Interfaces with the live environment

In order to establish whether transaction processing services have been available as agreed and whether batch work has been processed by agreed times the tool may need to interface to any automated scheduling tool in use.

Does the tool interface to the automated scheduler in use?

Some of the performance monitoring required by service level management may be performed by the base operating system or associated utility software (accounting data, system journals etc). The tool will need access to this data, so an interface will be needed.

Does the tool have an interface to performance data produced by components of the live environment?

7.2 Cost management

There are several interfaces required for the costing aspects of cost management, but this number will increase significantly if charging is also employed.

Interfaces with other infrastructure support tools

The cost management tool must interface with:

- service level management
- capacity management
- change management
- configuration management
- help desk/problem management.

Where charges are to be made for specific services, details of the service achievements will be needed to determine whether agreed levels have been met, or whether penalty payments are to be invoked. Details of charging formulae and criteria should be included in SLAs. There needs, therefore, to be close integration between cost management and service level management products.

Is there a close integration with service level management products?

Where charges are based upon resource usage, monitored usage data are needed to calculate charges. The tool must therefore interface with any capacity management monitoring tools in order to gather these data.

Is there an interface to capacity management resource monitoring facilities?

If charges are made for equipment held, the cost manager will need to access the CMDB to determine the equipment held by individuals or groups. The cost management tool should ideally be fully integrated with the CMDB, or at least offer a close interface (one that requires no manual intervention).

Details of capital costs and depreciation will also be needed from the CMDB when preparing budget estimates or financial statements.

Is the cost management tool fully integrated with the CMDB, or does it at least offer a close interface?

If charges are made for help desk and problem management support an interface is needed to these disciplines to determine the amount of support provided to individual customers or groups.

Is there an interface to help desk and problem management?

Interfaces with other tools being used within the organisation	It is essential that the cost management tool interfaces closely with the organisation's business accounting systems, particularly for those IT organisations that are run as a separate business centre, to allow accurate estimating and tracking of actual expenditure and income against estimates and to ensure that invoices raised for IT services are integrated into the overall business accounting systems.

Does the cost management tool integrate closely with the organisation's business accounting systems?

If charges are based upon staffing resources (eg time spend by help desk, software maintenance or operations staff), the cost management tool should integrate closely with the organisation's staff time recording system (and/or flexitime, clocking systems etc), to allow relevant charges to be calculated.

Does the tool integrate with the organisation's staff time recording system?

Interfaces with the live environment	Some of the resource usage data required by cost management may be performed by the base operating system or associated utility software. The tool will therefore need access to these data, so an interface will be needed.

Does the tool have an interface to resource usage data produced by components of the live environment?

7.3 Contingency planning

Many of the key external interfaces for the contingency planning tool will be with components of the live environments which the plan seeks to protect. There are, however, a number of other close interfaces required during the planning phases.

Interfaces with other infrastructure support tools	The contingency planning tool must interface with capacity management as well as the service support disciplines of configuration management and change management.

For risk analysis and resilience planning purposes it will be necessary to identify key components and services, business dependencies, risks and threats. A close interface will, therefore, be required to the CMDB where this information is held.

Does the tool have a close interface with the CMDB?

During resilience planning it will be helpful if it is possible to model the potential impact of proposed changes or upgrades to determine the likely effect, without having to incur the cost and potential disruption of implementation with uncertain results. If the tool has no integrated modelling capabilities, then interfaces to external modelling packages will be required.

Does the tool have interfaces to modelling packages allowing proposed resilience upgrades to be evaluated prior to implementation?

To determine the required size of back-up machines and communications equipment needed to protect the key services identified during a business impact analysis, interfaces to capacity management tools and techniques are required.

Does the tool offer interfaces to capacity management tools and techniques?

The potential impact of proposed changes upon the resilience of the IT infrastructure and upon the organisation's Business Continuity Plans must be assessed. The contingency planning manager must therefore be involved in the assessment process of all proposed changes and an interface is required with the organisations change management system. To save time and avoid delays, the two-way transfer of Requests for Change (RFCs) should ideally be managed electronically.

Is there an interface to the organisation's change management system, ideally managed electronically?

Interfaces with other tools being used within the organisation

Unless risk analysis and assessment capabilities are fully integrated into the tool, an interface will be required with external products of this type, such as CRAMM software (which many users may anyway wish to use as a standard).

Does the tool interface with external risk analysis and assessment packages, such as CRAMM?

The tool should interface with any media management product(s) being used by the organisation to ensure that adequate backup copies of all data are being made and to identify their locations should implementation or testing of contingency plans be required.

Is there an interface to any media management system(s) being used?

The tool should integrate software facilities to automatically restore back-up copies of the operational environment and all required data at a remote facility,

Chapter 7
Integration with other products

or have very close interfaces with external products of this type.

Does the tool integrate with, or have interfaces with, software facilities to automatically restore back-up copies of the operational environment and all required data at a remote location?

Interfaces with the live environment

If a disaster occurs it will be necessary to recover the total live environment, not just the applications and services that run within that environment. The tool must therefore have close interfaces with all aspects of the live environment that the Contingency Plan seeks to protect and, if necessary, restore should a disaster occur.

Does the tool have close interfaces with those aspects of the live environment which the Contingency Plan seeks to protect/restore?

7.4 Capacity management

It is likely that the capacity manager will need to deal with a wide ranging IT infrastructure made up of diverse equipment and technologies. The capacity management tool will therefore require a significant number of interfaces with the live environment, other service management products and development methods.

Interfaces with other infrastructure support tools

The capacity management tool must interface with service level management products as well as with tools to support the service support disciplines of configuration management and change management

In order to establish required performance information and expected user demand for services, such as anticipated transaction throughput rates, the tool should have access to the details included in Service Level Agreements. The capacity management tool must report back actual performance achievement to service level management. If support for these two disciplines is not fully integrated within the tool then close interfaces between separate support tools is essential.

Does the tool fully integrate capacity and service level management, or at least provide close interfaces between the two?

When building capacity management models or during sizing exercises, it will be essential to have details readily available of the components that make up the IT infrastructure, particularly hardware and communications items, their performance characteristics and throughput rates. Ready access to this information on the CDB (which ideally should be an integral part of the CMDB) will therefore be required.

Does the tool have ready access to the CMDB allowing information to be easily obtained for modelling or sizing purposes?

The potential impact of proposed changes upon the organisation's Capacity Plan must be assessed. The capacity manager must, therefore, be involved in the assessment process of all proposed changes and an interface is required with the organisation's change management system. To save time and avoid delays, the two-way transfer of Requests for Change (RFCs) should ideally be achieved electronically.

Is there an interface with the organisation's change management system, ideally achieved electronically?

Interfaces with other tools being used within the organisation

If the tool does not have fully integrated network monitoring and modelling capabilities, able to identify or predict throughput traffic and performance difficulties, it must provide interfaces with separate products of this type.

Does the tool have fully integrated network monitoring and modelling capabilities, or, as a minimum, provide interfaces with separate products of this type?

Where Computer Aided Software Testing (CAST) tools are being used in the software development cycle, there should be an interface with the capacity management tool to obtain early performance characteristics of applications under test.

Does the tool have an interface with any CAST tools?

Development methods such as SSADM for designing information systems, provide logical and physical design products which can be a valuable input to the capacity planning process to build workload models to predict the hardware requirements and performance of systems while they are being developed.

Is the tool able to utilise output from a structured development method?

Chapter 7
Integration with other products

If the tool does not incorporate a data storage management system which allows disc lay-outs to be planned in advance and incorporating modelling capabilities, then interfaces with external systems that provide these capabilities will be required.

Does the tool incorporate or have interfaces with facilities for planning and modelling data storage and in particular disc lay-outs?

Interfaces with the live environment

Some of the monitoring capabilities required by capacity management may be performed by the operating system or some other part of the live environment. In such cases the tool must interface to such monitoring systems in order to access the monitored data.

Does the tool interface with monitoring performed by the live environment?

7.5 Availability management

The major interfaces for the availability management tool are with service level management and the service support disciplines of help desk/problem management, configuration management and change management.

Interfaces with other infrastructure support tools

Availability will be a key aspect to be included in all SLAs. Once availability levels have been agreed they must be managed and monitored by availability management. There is therefore a need for a close interface with service level management tools

Does the tool have a close interface with service level management tools?

To assist in improving availability levels access will be needed with historical help desk and problem management data, in order to highlight trends and identify potential weaknesses.

Is there ready access to historical help desk and problem management data?

When planning for higher availability levels through increased resilience, it will be essential to have details readily available of the components that make up the IT infrastructure, together with associated historical information (such as inherent weaknesses, previous failure records and known errors). Ready access to this information on the CMDB will therefore be required.

Does the tool have ready access to the CMDB allowing information to be easily obtained for planning higher availability through increased resilience?

The potential impact of proposed changes upon availability levels must be assessed. The availability manager must, therefore, be involved in the assessment process of all proposed changes and an interface is required with the organisation's change management system. To save time and avoid delays, the two-way transfer of Requests for Change (RFCs) should ideally be achieved electronically.

Is there an interface with the organisation's change management system?

Interfaces with other tools being used within the organisation	If the tool does not fully integrate event alerting and management capabilities, interfaces will be required with external systems capable of error detection and, where possible, correction in order to minimise downtime and improve availability levels.

Does the tool fully integrate or have close interfaces with event alerting and management facilities capable of error detection and, where possible, correction?

If the tool does not incorporate resilience and availability modelling capabilities, interfaces with external products with these capabilities will be required.

Does the tool incorporate or have interfaces with external products with resilience and availability modelling capabilities?

Interfaces with the live environment	Some of the availability monitoring requirements may be met by the operating system or other aspects of the live environment. In such cases ready access will be required to obtain this data.

Are any availability monitoring data produced within the live environment readily accessible?

Part 3
Annexes

A Criteria hierarchy

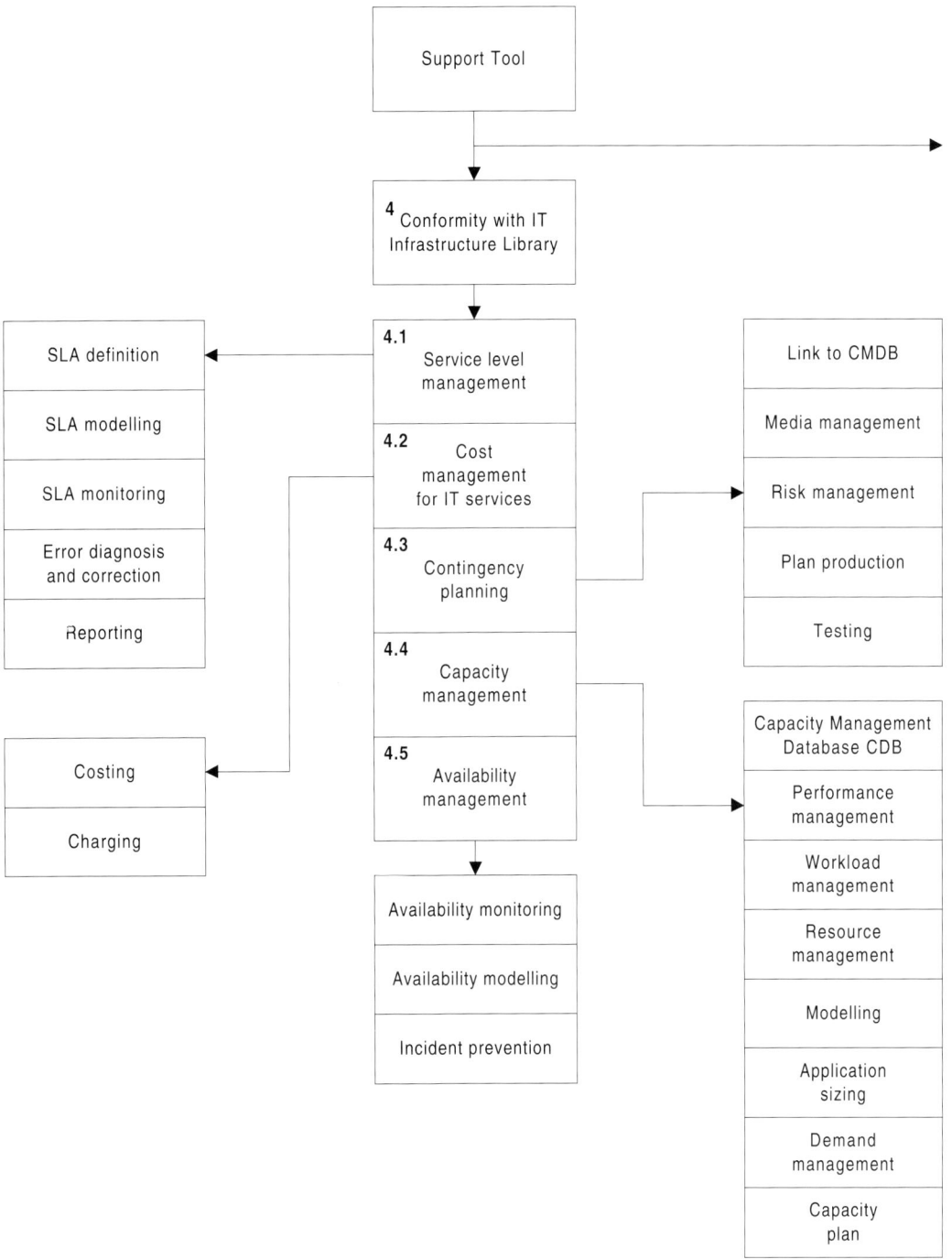

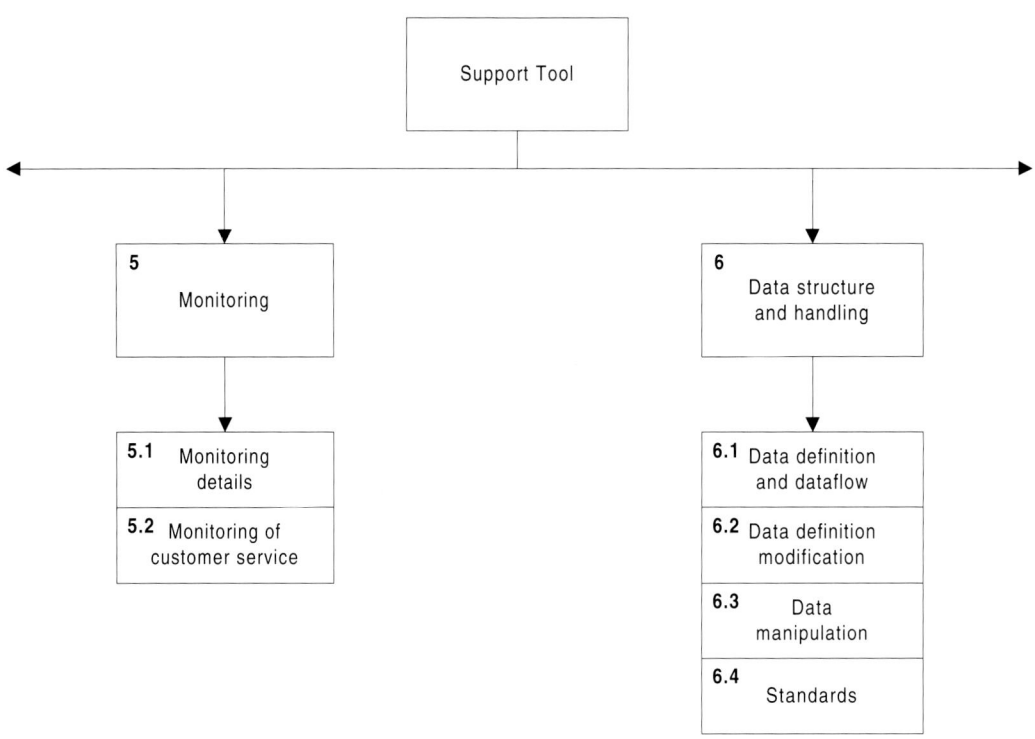

Annex A
Criteria hierarchy

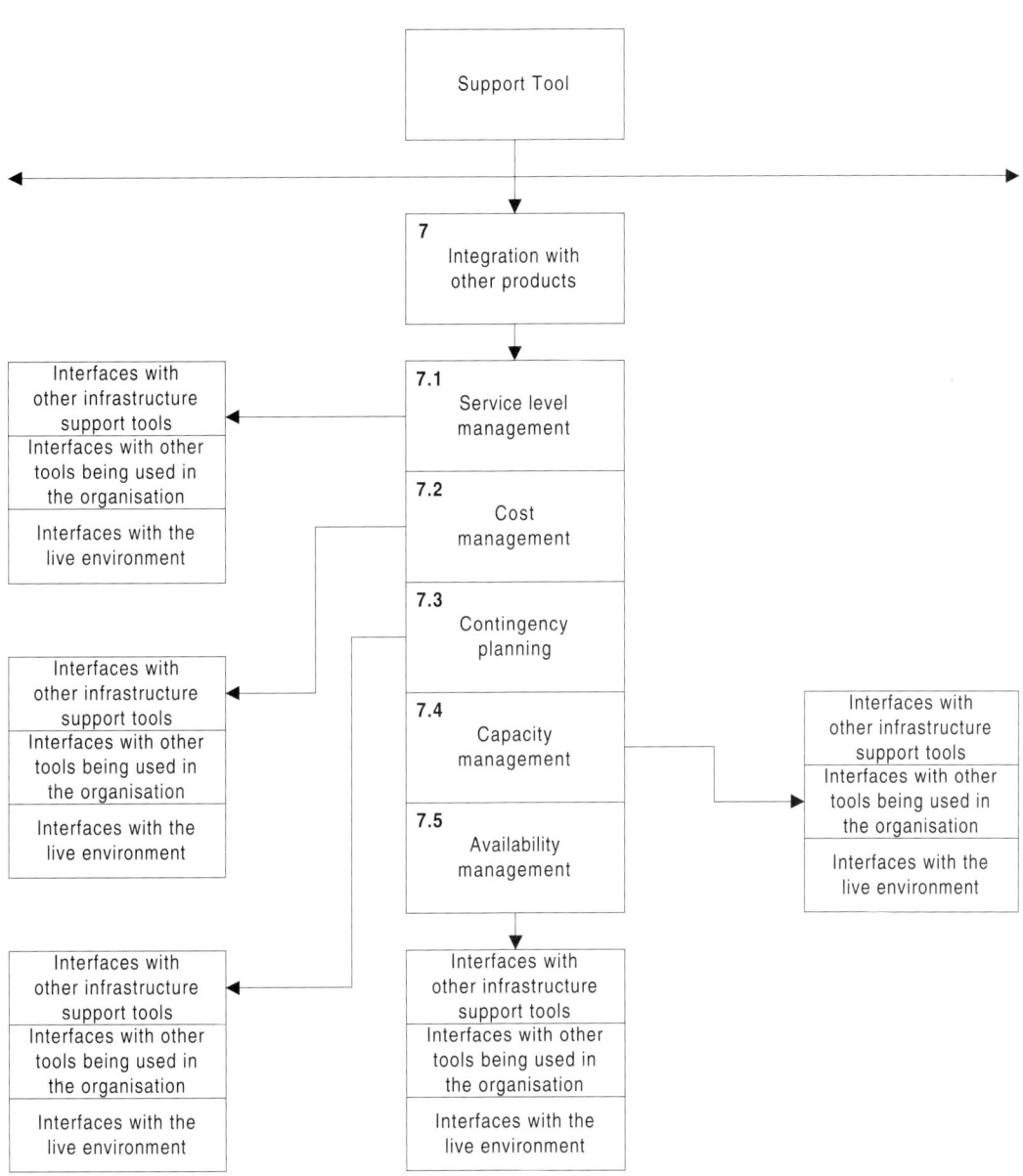

B Evaluation checklist

This section lists the criteria detailed within this volume, that can form the basis of an operational requirement. The side headings indicate the chapter and section within the volume where detailed information may be found.

B.1 Conformity with the IT Infrastructure Library

Are all mandatory requirements met?

Does the application meet at least 80 per cent of the functional requirements (mandatory and desirable) as stated in the OR?

Service level management

Does the tool incorporate, or have close interfaces with, word processing capabilities?

Does the tool provide a skeleton SLA and 'standard sections'?

Is the tool flexible enough to meet individual needs?

Does the tool have an integrated modelling capability or provide close interfaces with external modelling package(s)?

Is it possible to set thresholds against service achievements?

What degree of automated error diagnosis and resolution is possible?

What level and content of diagnostic information can be provided to assist manual resolution?

Does the tool provide adequate exception and periodic reporting facilities?

Is it capable of aggregating data from many sources to give a co-ordinated picture?

Does the tool support the production of graphical summaries including highlighting breaches of thresholds?

Is it possible to tailor reports to specific audiences?

Cost management for IT services

Does the tool provide integrated spreadsheet capabilities to allow budget estimates and actual expenditure to be captured and managed?

Does the spreadsheet provide sufficient capacity and accuracy for the organisation's needs?

Is there an interface with invoice payment systems to capture actual expenditure data automatically?

Does the tool allow different currency data entry, storage and automatic conversion?

	Where relevant, can the tool interface to applications software to obtain business transaction data?
	Is the tool able to normalise data arriving from applications in differing formats?
	Does the tool provide a close interface to a Configuration Management Database?
	What degree of automated support does the tool provide for dealing with depreciation?
	Does the tool support a full range of charging options and allow for differential charging using user defined algorithms?
	What degree of financial modelling does the tool provide to calculate expected outturn?
	Does the tool enable a complete and up-to-date picture of equipment held and network connectivity to be maintained and used for charging purposes?
	Does the tool allow automated calculation of prices, and total charges based on monitored data, for business transactions?
	Does the tool allow automatic apportionment in accordance with a predefined ratio or formula?
	Does the tool allow staff time-recording and calculation of charges to be made for staff time?
	Does the tool allow monitoring of SLA breaches to enable credit payments to be calculated and made?
	Does the tool calculate and produce itemised statements, invoices, reminders and credit notes for the appropriate people or groups?
	Does the tool incorporate an accounting spreadsheet capable of supporting double-entry bookkeeping and to allow production of a balance sheet and profit/loss accounts?
Contingency planning	*Does the tool provide a link to an integrated CMDB, or failing that some form of suitable inventory, to assist in business impact, risk and resilience analysis?*
	Does the tool include, or provide an interface with, a media management system capable of maintaining a complete and up-to-date record of all back-up security copies and their locations?
	Does the tool support transmission of security copies direct to remote locations, with acknowledgement capabilities?

Does the tool support periodic audits to determine if all data and media are held as expected?

Does the tool provide an interface with CRAMM or some equivalent risk analysis and management product?

Does the tool include word processing and graphical facilities allowing a Contingency Plan to be quickly produced from a predefined skeleton and 'standard sections'?

Is a complete record of the location and owner of each copy of the Contingency Plan readily available?

Is there easy access to the DSL and CMDB?

What support is provided for testing the Contingency Plan?

Capacity management

Does the tool include a Capacity Management Database (CDB) and is this fully integrated to the CMDB?

Does the tool incorporate expert system performance analysis and automated tuning recommendations?

Does the tool allow workload details and characteristics to be held as part of the CDB (ideally as an integral part of the CMDB)?

Is ready access to service and customer information on the CMDB available to allow initial identification of workloads?

Does the tool allow ready access to monitored performance data for workload management purposes?

Does the tool incorporate or have interfaces with facilities for planning and modelling data storage and in particular disc lay-outs?

Does the tool incorporate easy to use modelling capabilities and have access to device and network performance and throughput criteria, ideally via the CMDB?

Is there an automated link to monitored performance data and is it possible to calibrate and amend models easily and quickly?

Does the tool have comprehensive reporting facilities?

Does the tool provide specialist modelling capabilities to allow sizing of new applications?

Are there links with the application lifecycle, ideally via the CMDB, which trigger the need for further sizing work?

Is easy access provided to business information held in the CMDB?

		Does the tool provide easy access to work scheduling software to allow implementation of any required restrictions?
		Does the tool incorporate word processing facilities and include a 'skeleton' Capacity Plan?
		Is there easy access to the DSL and CMDB?
	Availability management	*Does the tool allow service availability, as perceived by the customers, to be monitored?*
		Does the tool allow incidents caused by third parties to be identified?
		Does the tool incorporate resilience and availability modelling capabilities and have ready access to CMDB relationship, dependency and historical failure information?
		Does the tool incorporate or have close links to event monitoring software?
		Is it possible to set thresholds and raise alerts if these are exceeded?
		Can the tool assess events and perform automated preventative action where this can be predefined?
		Is the tool capable of calling for human intervention, offering a range of options depending upon the impact and severity of the event?
B.2	**Monitoring**	*Is the tool capable of gathering and filtering monitored data from all required technical environments and normalising and storing this in a centralised location where it can be used by all service delivery applications?*
		Does the tool run on a dedicated platform, making it independent of the environments being monitored?
		Is the tool capable of controlling the parameters of host monitors to manage the frequency and format of monitored data?
		Is it possible to 'timetable' the level of monitoring?
		Is it possible to report on individual transactions and/or transaction types with different targets for individual users?
		Are data stored and reported in such a way that trends are easily identified?
	Monitoring details	*Is the tool capable of monitoring all the elements mentioned in Figure 4?*

	Monitoring of customer service	*Does the tool allow availability, reliability, and response time monitoring 'at the terminal' for all terminals connected to network?*
		If 'at the terminal' monitoring is not available for all terminals, is there a sampling ability capable of accurately assessing terminal response times?
		If 'at the terminal' monitoring, or sampling, is not available, does the tool allow close monitoring of computers and networks to measure terminal response times with reasonable accuracy?
		Does the tool have access to the help desk and CMDB?
		Is the tool able to access performance and availability data as monitored and recorded by the help desk?
B.3	**Data structure and handling**	*Can logical data definitions be enhanced and modified without extensive changes to the physical database definition?*
	Data definition and dataflow	*What constraints are there in making changes to the logical data structure?*
		Does the tool's underlying database support the use of application specific views?
		Is there sufficient data independence to make it possible to reorganise data as needed to meet changing requirements?
		Does the tool allow the user to define data types and valid data ranges?
		Does the proposed database implementation allow modification of storage structures?
		Can the tool support the storage and rapid retrieval of free text?
	Data definition modification	*What database restructuring facilities exist?*
		Is it possible to add, delete and rename data items and change the relationships between record types?
		What facilities exist to improve performance?
		Can restructuring take place while the application is still running?
		What utilities are available to assist restructuring?
	Data manipulation	*What user defined query functionality is supported?*
	Standards	*Is the database structure based on accepted standards?*

What degree of conformity to this standard is supported and what, if any, proprietary additions have been made?

Does the tool's data definition and manipulation language conform to the organisation's standards?

B.4 Integration with other products

Service level management

If no integrated modelling exists, does the tool have an interface with capacity management modelling facilities?

Does the tool integrate with, or allow close interfaces to, help desk and problem management tools?

Does the tool interface with cost management system(s) to allow credit payments to be triggered?

Does the tool have interfaces with contingency planning information so that service levels following a disaster can be determined?

Does the tool have a direct interface with change management and the CMDB?

Is there a link to tools that support the development method, such as CASE tools, to allow SLR data to be exchanged?

If necessary, is there an interface with network management tools?

Does the tool interface with the automated scheduler in use?

Does the tool have an interface with performance data produced by components of the live environment?

Cost management

Is there a close integration with service level management products?

Is there an interface with capacity management resource monitoring facilities?

Is the cost management tool fully integrated with the CMDB, or does it at least offer a close interface?

Is there an interface with help desk and problem management?

Does the cost management tool integrate closely with the organisation's Business Accounting Systems?

Does the tool integrate with the organisation's staff time recording system?

	Does the tool have an interface with resource usage data produced by components of the live environment?
Contingency planning	*Does the tool have a close interface with the CMDB?*
	Does the tool have interfaces with modelling packages allowing proposed resilience upgrades to be evaluated prior to implementation?
	Does the tool offer interfaces with capacity management tools and techniques?
	Is there an interface with the organisation's change management system, ideally managed electronically?
	Does the tool interface with external risk analysis and assessment packages, such as CRAMM?
	Is there an interface with any media-management system(s) being used?
	Does the tool integrate with, or have interfaces to, software facilities to automatically restore back-up copies of the operational environment and all required data at a remote location?
	Does the tool have close interfaces with those aspects of the live environment that the Contingency Plan seeks to protect/restore?
Capacity management	*Does the tool fully integrate capacity and service level management, or at least provide close interfaces between the two?*
	Does the tool have ready access to the CMDB allowing information to be easily obtained for modelling or sizing purposes?
	Is there an interface with the organisation's change management system, ideally achieved electronically?
	Does the tool fully integrate network monitoring and modelling capabilities, or as a minimum provide interfaces with separate products of this type?
	Does the tool have an interface with any CAST tools?
	Does the tool incorporate or have interfaces with facilities for planning and modelling data storage and in particular disc layouts?
	Does the tool interface with monitoring performed by the live environment?

Availability management

Does the tool have a close interface with service level management tools?

Is there ready access to historical help desk and problem management data?

Does the tool have ready access to the CMDB allowing information to be easily obtained for planning higher availability through increased resilience?

Is there an interface with the organisation's change management system, ideally achieved electronically?

Does the tool fully integrate or have close interfaces with event alerting and management facilities capable of error detection and, where possible, correction?

Does the tool incorporate or have interfaces with external products with resilience and availability modelling capabilities?

Are any availability monitoring data produced within the live environment readily accessible?

C Glossary

ANSI	American National Standards Institute.
CASE	Computer Aided Systems Engineering.
CAST	Computer Aided Software Testing.
CCTA	The Government Centre for Information Systems.
CDB	Capacity Management Database.
CI	Configuration Item.
CMDB	Configuration Management Database.
CPU	Central Processing Unit.
CRAMM	CCTA Risk Analysis and Management Method.
DBMS	Database Management System.
DDE	Microsoft Windows Direct Data Exchange system.
DSL	Definitive Software Library.
I/O	Input/Output.
ISO	International Organisation for Standardisation.
IT	Information Technology.
ITIMF	IT Infrastructure Management Forum.
MTBF	Mean Time Between Failures.
OLE	Microsoft Windows Object Linking Environment.
OR	Operational Requirement.
OSI	Open Systems Interconnection; a set of standard communication protocols based upon a seven layer reference model.
RFC	Request for Change.
SC&D	Software Control and Distribution.
SLA	Service Level Agreement.
SLR	Service Level Requirement.
SQL	Structured Query Language.
SSADM	Structured Systems Analysis and Design Method.

Printed in the United Kingdom for HMSO
Dd302016 2/96 C8 G3397 10170